CAPITALISM XXL

CAPITALISM XXL

Why the Global Economy
Became Gigantic and How to Fix It

GEERT NOELS

McGill-Queen's University Press
Montreal & Kingston · London · Chicago

© McGill-Queen's University Press 2023

Originally published in Dutch as *Gigantisme: Van too big to fail naar trager, kleiner en menselijker* © Lannoo Publishers, 2019

www.lannoo.com

ISBN 978-0-2280-1690-8 (cloth)
ISBN 978-0-2280-1854-4 (ePDF)
ISBN 978-0-2280-1855-1 (ePUB)

Legal deposit second quarter 2023
Bibliothèque nationale du Québec

Printed in Canada on acid-free paper that is 100% ancient forest free (100% post-consumer recycled), processed chlorine free

Library and Archives Canada Cataloguing in Publication

Title: Capitalism XXL : why the global economy became gigantic and how to fix it / Geert Noels.

Names: Noels, Geert, 1967– author.

Description: Includes bibliographical references and index.

Identifiers: Canadiana (print) 20230154662 | Canadiana (ebook) 20230154735 | ISBN 9780228016908 (cloth) | ISBN 9780228018551 (ePUB) | ISBN 9780228018544 (ePDF)

Subjects: LCSH: Capitalism. | LCSH: Capitalism – Social aspects. | LCSH: Capitalism – Environmental aspects. | LCSH: Sustainable development.

Classification: LCC HB501 .N64 2023 | DDC 330.12/2 – dc23

This book was designed and typeset by Peggy & Co. Design in 11/14 Adobe Minion Pro.

C'était un cordonnier, sans rien d'particulier.
Dans un village dont le nom m'a échappé.
Qui faisait des souliers si jolis, si légers.
Que nos vies semblaient un peu moins lourdes à porter.
Il y mettait du temps, du talent et du cœur.
Ainsi passait sa vie au milieu de nos heures.
Et loin des beaux discours, des grandes théories.
A sa tâche chaque jour, on pouvait dire de lui.
Il changeait la vie.
JEAN-JACQUES GOLDMAN

Any intelligent fool can make things bigger, more complex, and more violent. It takes a touch of genius – and a lot of courage to move in the opposite direction.

Perhaps we cannot raise the winds. But each of us can put up the sail, so that when the wind comes, we can catch it.
ERNST FRIEDRICH SCHUMACHER

Problems cannot be solved at the same level of consciousness that created them.
ALBERT EINSTEIN

If you think you're too small to make a difference, you've probably never spent the night with a mosquito in your room.
PROVERB

CONTENTS

CAPITALISM XXL

INTRODUCTION

More than a decade after the financial crisis, and as many years after the publication of my book *Econoshock*, it is time to analyze the world economy anew – now from a different point of view. In *Econoshock* I started with long-term trends and identified six major shifts, each of which had caused a significant system shock. As the six shocks coincided, they sparked a huge and rarely seen shock to the world economy. In 2008, I called this event, comparable only to the industrial revolution, "Econoshock." In 2023 the World Economic Forum talks about the polycrisis, and others about the "age of disruption." The six shocks coalesced around six major axes:

- Demographics: the aging population, together with megacities, the demographic decline of Europe, the rise of Africa, the concentration in Asia, and the growth of the total world population.
- Energy: the end of the fossil fuel era and the search for renewable energy sources and efficiency; the creation of a worldwide energy web.
- Economic centres of gravity: the rise of China in particular, and a different economic power balance between the traditional economic blocs and the "emerging economies"; the relative decline of Europe and its impact on trade and power relations.
- Climate: underexposed in 2008; global warming caused by greenhouse gas emissions, and the underestimation of their consequences due to the inertia of our blue planet.
- Technology: the massive technological disruptions, which in 2008 were just the start of what we now call exponential technological changes.

- Financial system: this shock received full attention in 2008, but is ultimately just one of six shocks that took place, albeit with far-reaching consequences; the unsustainability of big banks; the dangers of a rigid euro and an expanding eurozone; the ever-growing debt problems and money printing.

These six shocks could more accurately be labelled macroeconomic in nature. They are major trends, long-term movements that shape the entire economy and our society. Today, *Econoshock* and the six trends remain highly topical. Today there is (fortunately) far greater emphasis on climate challenges. There are varying degrees of concern about the financial system, but an inevitable new financial crisis awaits us in the years ahead or is already brewing. After all, we have tackled only the symptoms, not the causes. An update to *Econoshock* would make sense, but there is far more to it than that. Hence the need to examine events from a different angle. How have our organizations changed? What stands out when we look at companies, at how competition is handled, or at how the state runs the economy? This analysis starts more from a microeconomic perspective (that of companies, institutions, or other organizations) but rapidly offers insights into how the economy is organized today. It becomes evident that scale is massively encouraged, and we are witnessing the emergence of ever-larger companies and organizations – developments that I believe have a common cause and can be labelled "gigantism." I admit that this is a simple concept, but it is a highly complex system with innumerable facets. Gigantism is not yet an economic concept; today it is mainly used in the medical world to refer to a condition that causes abnormal growth in people. Intuitively one understands that it refers to size, to things that are not only big but too big. Similar to what we see in the natural world, other organisms can also become oversized – not only economic organizations but political entities, too. In turn, this affects the shapes of buildings, ships, and aircraft, which grow along with them, driven by prestige, necessity, or a combination of the two. For now, let us ignore the fact that egos and potentates tend to grow alongside as a result.

Gigantism is caused by a combination of many factors. We need to identify them to understand how the situation gradually got out of hand before escalating exponentially. Only then can we think about real solutions to the crisis and to the emergencies with which we have yet to deal. The solution to this phenomenon will make the economic and financial systems far more sustainable and other aspects of our society healthier.

The financial crisis in 2008 was only one dimension of a more widespread malaise. The ecological and demographic derailments are other sides of the same phenomenon. This brings us back to the basic premise of *Econoshock*: several parallel changes are currently at play. Because of the way we stimulate the world economy, our impact on it is huge. If we want to tackle financial instability, we will have to make the too-big-to-fail banks smaller. A solution to climate and energy problems is exceedingly complex but also forces us to think in a more decentralized way. Many of our diseases of affluence are treated chemically, while the root cause of many is the lost chemistry between people.

The COVID-19 crisis gave gigantism an enormous boost. Technology companies enjoyed an extra growth shot; big pharma and big government also made an extra quantum leap. Yet, it also sparked a countermovement: the search and demand for more attention to local production, for instance, out of necessity due to a broken logistics system, out of safety, and out of renewed attention to the human connection.

In 2021 one of the world's largest container ships, *Ever Given*, became stuck in the Suez Canal, giving the world economy a heart attack. It prompted an opinion piece in the leading Dutch financial newspaper by the Dutch economist Mathijs Bouman, in which he spurred me to write an update of the book, with the gigaship on the new book's cover. I did, and the image graces the back cover. This cardiac arrest was no coincidence, however; sooner or later the world economy was bound to run aground in the vulnerability of its quest for never-ending economies of scale. It is important to not only point out problems but also to think about solutions. That is the role of opinion makers and policy-makers. We must ensure that the crisis does not lead us into making the wrong choices and plunging our economy and society into a deeper and longer-lasting crisis.

Policy-makers today are not always aware of their tunnel vision. "Growth is good," they say, and, to some extent, that is correct. Extra growth should help us out of the crisis, they say. To some degree, that is also correct. But from a certain level this statement no longer holds true. Excessive growth, or unsustainable growth, exacerbates debt and climate problems. And to be precise, sustainable economic growth can be achieved without making organizations, companies, or powers larger. Policy-makers are often proponents of centralizing power and decision making: create bigger entities to solve world problems "because alone we are too small." That is wrong! Numerous world problems can be dealt with in a far more decentralized fashion. The large COVID-19 rescue funds will lead to considerable corruption, inefficiency and, yes, gigantism. And what about the climate problems or the plastic soup? For those, surely we need a huge, global approach? These problems became out of hand precisely because we thought big and allowed gigantism to creep into the rules of our economy. If we misunderstand the problems, then we will, of course, propose the wrong solutions. Countless problems would be smaller if we did not always think big. We need to reacquire this skill.

Some of the world's major issues are also best tackled decentrally and on a small scale: recycling, waste separation, local production, and conscious consumerism. The climate will be saved not by big agreements alone but more by conscious people and ingenious scientists.

Another risk is the repudiation of growth. COVID-19 and renewed climate concerns are fuelling a trend towards renouncing growth. But that, too, is unwise. Growth is simply the translation of the inherent human ambition to move forward, to seek solutions, and to be creative and resourceful. The solution to climate or energy challenges is the economic growth of tomorrow. We also need growth in order to repay debts, keep health affordable, and further eradicate poverty. *Degrowth* is not a philosophy but a statement that proves people do not understand what sustainable growth really means and what always drives people: the desire to improve things. Degrowth will lead to declining living standards, poverty, and ultimately chaos.

The search for the right balance between growth and the size of organizations, between centralization and decentralization, and between globalization and localism are all topics that are addressed here. The more involved people are, the happier they become, and the more responsible is their use of raw materials and resources.

The crucial issue that concerns me is how to restore the economy's health – for people, the government, the community, and the planet. This is not simply a question for economists; we must not think one dimensionally. For that matter, it is far from an economic issue; it touches all aspects of our society and even our humanity. That is why, as an economist, I am eager to learn from other disciplines such as sociology, natural sciences, sports, and politics. Nature teaches us the ways in which things that go off the rails eventually achieve a new balance. Sports teach us much about the dynamics of how people can achieve a goal together. Hence, sports remain a mirror of the economy and society. The same applies to games, such as Monopoly, Uno, or chess. They say something about freedom within certain rules and how we can adapt our behaviour accordingly, take risks, or cooperate. Politics will have to learn to reinvent itself, to give up power to lower entities, to intervene less, and to invest more trust in citizens and entrepreneurs who pursue a well-managed self-interest and thereby better serve the common good.

If you believe that the exaggerations are only economic, you need to expand your view considerably. For me, it is overly clear that the obsession with growth has translated into ecological and social imbalances. We cannot get a grip on these imbalances because the proposed solutions only move us further away from the balance. Unfortunately many of the solutions are far too ideologically tinted. Too left-wing, for example, as in, "Economy is bad, capital is bad, corporations are the source of all evil." Or too right-wing, as in, "More leadership is needed"; or, "There is no climate crisis, capitalism will save everything, entrepreneurs can solve all world problems." A more balanced approach to ideologies is also needed. We must learn that valuable points bubble up on both sides of the ideological spectrum.

To change people's behaviour you must convince them and give them subtle incentives to steer them in the right direction. But the rules of the global economy must not override these positive incentives. This is precisely where the shoe pinches today. If the world economy were a giant computer-simulation game, the operating system would be jammed now and in need of a reset.

So we embark on a bold thought exercise. The current solutions are widely supported by the powers that be: political, institutional, and corporate. Change provokes resistance, and human beings do not embrace change unless they are convinced it is for the better. This change will not be managed from the top, which has too much to lose from it; on the contrary, to be successful, it will have to come from below, bottom-up, and step by step.

This bottom-up change is already the case in other areas: commitments to clean technology or decent working conditions, and the fight against poverty or for a better environment, do not come from the established structures. They are achieved day by day, little by little, bottom-up, through the behaviour of all the people who believe in them. If we can give that process a little push, an acceleration, then we all become activists for a people-sized economy. That is the economy I wish to promote by offering fresh ideas. That is what drove me to write *Capitalism XXL*. At a time when voices call to abolish capitalism, renounce growth, and intensify government involvement as solutions to the challenges and crises, I argue for the renunciation of fake capitalism and a return to the humane capitalism that Adam Smith also envisioned.

THE WORLD ECONOMY
AND CAPITALISM ADRIFT
Adam Smith versus John Maynard Keynes

Confidence in capitalism has been badly damaged. No wonder that countless taxpayers doubt the system when it is their money that saves capitalism during a financial crisis – especially when disaster strikes in an era of million-dollar bonuses for bankers, and big banks have grown so large that people feel they cannot and should not be allowed to fail. The current climate catastrophe is eroding this confidence even further. The enormous emission of greenhouse gases can be traced to a hundred or so large capitalist corporations.[1] Thus, it comes as no surprise that people are calling into question a system that has allowed such players to disrupt the climate indiscriminately, thereby affecting every human being on the planet, perhaps most of all the weakest, who are unable to reap the full benefits of this capitalist system. Although the introduction of state capitalism in China lifted many people out of poverty, today's capitalism is rightly – but also often wrongly – linked to poverty, inequality, and other injustices.

A number of economists who have a growing following among the media and the general public are therefore seriously questioning or rejecting capitalism. There is an increasing number of economists who advocate a certain form of far-reaching socialism that tends towards communism, with a dominant role for government. The work of the French economist Thomas Piketty (*Capital in the Twenty-First Century*) sees capitalism as an inherent source of injustice. He claims that capitalism makes the rich richer because the rate of return on capital in the long run outstrips the rate of economic growth.[2] Not only are the time series on which Piketty relies impossible to interpret unambiguously, but capital is not the same as wealth. Other economists make a show of wanting to preserve capitalism but undermine its very essence: for example, by giving the government a dominant role or by proposing alternative money theories that take the process of risk and return, efficient allocation of scarce resources, and productive investment away from individuals and organizations and entrust it to governments and, to be more precise, central banks.

Central planning is an experiment that is doomed to fail. The more we plan centrally, the more people and society will feel passed over. Complex systems cannot be centrally planned. Furthermore, economics that pays no heed to social factors results in huge imbalances that will be felt far beyond the purely economic field: climate issues, inequality, diseases of affluence, and the like.

The central line that I advance in this book advocates not rejecting capitalism but returning to its essence and to the ethical and social rules of play that were envisaged at its inception, or, if you like, by founding fathers such as Adam Smith (1723–1790) in particular. Smith's moral philosophy served as the framework on which he based his healthy principles and rules of play for early capitalism. He understood that people were largely motivated by their immediate social circle, by self-interest. But Smith also knew that one could achieve more for the common good by utilizing ethical insights to steer that self-interest than by imposing rigid government intervention that would stifle any initiative. Entrepreneurs needed to be encouraged to develop an ethical awareness, and, above all, government had to realize that it had to curb some of the processes that would derail capitalism. This was a simple framework in a period of nascent capitalism.

Adam Smith pointed to two main sources of derailment that would lead to bad capitalism:

- The formation of monopolies or oligopolies; in other words, the lack of competition and the formation of cartels.
- Too short a distance between government and business, an entanglement of the two, leading to "crony capitalism"; specifically, too much influence of lobby groups, powerful entrepreneurs or companies, all kinds of business clubs or other organizations, which can steer the public rules to the advantage of the incumbents at the expense of competition, innovation, and new entrants.

It is interesting to note that while Smith acknowledged the importance of the financial sector, he was not convinced that it really contributed to the overall economy. He considered it to be a form of rent-seeking.[3] So, from the start, there were warnings that, if it did not permanently monitor these two risks, capitalism would derail and become unfair. This is precisely what has happened in the past decades: there has been a strong concentration in various sectors, and powerful groups and companies have gained such a hold on governments (also internationally) that they have a hand in shaping legislation, obviously to their advantage.

We cannot emphasize enough that economics has no laws but must be considered above all as comprising agreements between players who optimize certain objectives within an agreed framework (e.g., ethical; sustainable; minimizing externalities; fair competition). Each school of economic thought therefore has its pros and cons but must also be evaluated against the agreements that citizens have made with their government. All those schools lead to completely different behaviours and thrive best if they are attuned to a certain culture that the population also embraces. A one-size-fits-all economic theory is therefore difficult, although a certain minimum framework is still acceptable and even desirable internationally.

Adam Smith clearly departed from a moral framework and from an analysis of human behaviour. How can "selfish" individuals be allowed to pursue self-interest, yet serve the common good? This was something that concerned Smith. He did not want to cripple private initiative; the creativity, entrepreneurship, and tremendous progress afforded by the ideas and initiatives of individuals and private organizations created vast wealth and solutions to long-standing problems. At the same time, however, Smith realized that individuals and organizations had the capacity to be immoral. For this reason, an individual moral framework, as well as a clear corporate framework, is essential to prevent capitalism's unwelcome excesses.

Gigantism affects the excesses. Adam Smith would have shuddered at the current economic framework, in which competition is inhibited by quasi-monopolies and enormous power positions. Equally, he would have protested against the power of lobby groups and entrepreneurs in the highest cenacles of political power. Rather than place private initiative and a moral framework at its centre, the current system favours existing positions of power. A problematic issue is rent-seeking, in which companies use the privileged position they have negotiated by political means to gain an advantage and thereby pocket a relatively risk-free "economic interest." Rent-seeking can also be defined more broadly as a way of boosting one's own value without creating value for the economy.

The economic system is drifting too far away from people and the interests of society. As a result, corporatist interests prevail, and politics becomes too much of an economic actor. This is precisely the problem at the heart of today's European economic system. Europe's system has wandered far from healthy capitalism. It has evolved from a capitalist system, to a mixed system with significant social corrections and government initiative, to a model of gigantism: ever-larger companies, organizations, lobby groups, and governments, which stifle citizens, entrepreneurship, and society. In the European Union (EU) the government has become too big; in the United States some companies and lobby groups have become too big. In both cases this gigantism stands in the way of the healthy capitalism that endows society with positive benefits.

The process has been underway for decades, and maybe the derailment (possibly unintentional) can be ascribed to the influence and insights of that other important economist, John Maynard Keynes (1883–1946). He reached his peak more than a century after Adam Smith, at another important pivotal moment: the Great Depression, followed by the Second World War. As in many other periods, economists sometimes make the mistake of believing that the economy is at a dead end and that major interventions are needed. By the 1920s, Keynes had already stopped believing in the need for "perfect competition," something that Smith, of course, considered essential. Keynes was not unsettled by the trend in that decade towards cartels, conglomerates, large companies (we would now say giants), and all kinds of trade organizations and interest groups, agreements, and monopolies; quite the contrary. He saw the merits of a government that sought to make a rapid impact and wished to do so by regulating the economy.[4]

So when Keynes announced the end of Smithian capitalism, or "the death of laissez-faire," in the 1920s, not only was he thinking of macroeconomic considerations but he also wanted the government to take control of and steer industrial policy. In many ways Keynes was the first economist to change the rules of capitalism in favour of gigantism. Is it any wonder that today's neo-Keynesian politics produces the same outcome? As Keynes enjoyed greater power and prestige, his ideas became more drastic. The British economist believed in the guiding role of economists and their models. It gave him considerable power, but it also gave governments additional regulatory functions and they consequently became a fan of his insights. This is still apparent today: economists who embrace Keynes tend to believe that an economy should be guided by models and the government, with economists at the helm. Keynes started as a mathematician, which explains his love of models and the belief that the economic system would follow certain equations in a predictable way. The result today, for example, is that central banks become the executors of Keynesian ideology, with powerful, non-democratically elected managers (usually, but not exclusively, economists) who are independent of political intervention but not politically unbiased.

Keynes was not in favour of perfect competition because he felt that consumers and the economy as a whole would lose out on a number of benefits as a result. Of course, "perfect competition" is a potential source of these downsides, but in practice it does not exist in the real world. Although Keynes is best known for his ideas on deficit spending and more government intervention during crises, he was also a corporatist (as explained earlier), especially in the late 1920s when corporate giants dominated the American economy. For example, there were three large automobile companies at the time, and the automobile sector was one of the most important branches of industry, somewhat similar to the tech sector today.

The American economist Edmund Phelps examined Keynes's theories and concluded that the oligopoly in branches such as the automobile sector could be explained by Keynes's belief in the strength of large corporations.[5] As a result, innovation took a back seat. Perhaps the electric car, which was already known in the late nineteenth century, would not have been neglected and reinvented until after the millennium if there had been more competition at that time! Keynes was also convinced that corporatism would better enable the government to steer the economy in the direction it wanted.

Keynes's ideas had more well-intentioned but undesirable effects on economic macro events. Top-down adjustment always starts with good intentions but quickly leads to excesses, imbalances, and the need for even more adjustments, resulting in new overshooting and ultimately in continuous interventions such as we see today in all parts of the world economy. Yet none of these governments foresaw the major crises looming on the horizon, and their so-called solutions were nothing more than interventions with which they could buy time (kicking the can down the road, as it were).

The fact that we see so many giants in the corporate world today, while at the same time we are confronted with a drop in productivity and abnormal profit margins in some companies, suggests that something is indeed fundamentally wrong. Competition is not working; there is insufficient innovation because small companies are bought up too quickly by large multinationals or are driven out, and the giants make huge but logical quasi-monopolistic profits.

There is no level playing field. Both the economist Friedrich Von Hayek (1899–1992)[6] and the historian and economist Deirdre McCloskey are liberal thinkers,[7] but they are opposed to concentration and oligopolies. Particularly undesirable are the monopolies and oligopolies promoted by state intervention or regulation. This rent-seeking, gaining a permanent advantage through expedient political contacts, is also called "political interest." It is at the expense of society and of fair entrepreneurship.

So, it is neither neo-liberalism nor neo-capitalism that is the problem today, as this system is more like fake capitalism: capitalism that no longer respects its own rules. Enterprises grow far larger than they would normally be in a well-functioning capitalist system because of a lack of competition or because of the benefits they receive from lobbying or their close contacts with the government. Smithian thinkers insist on the importance of involving "everyone" in the creative process, not just a protected or corporatist elite – every individual and every talent, from the top to the bottom of the organization and society. This factor, over the past few centuries, has also been at the root of the enormous growth in prosperity in the West. Innovation is not just about big inventions but also about all the know-how and small improvements that motivated employees bring to the production process. In order for this innovation to occur, an organization must be sufficiently decentralized that each employee feels involved and responsible. This is extremely difficult, if not impossible, to achieve in huge companies or public services. As a result, we miss out on a great deal of economic potential. And for the same reason, employees no longer feel involved.

The problem with corporatism is that it restricts entrepreneurship. Entrepreneurs have to jump through more and more hoops and obtain approval from the government, social partners, guilds, sector federations, licensing authorities, and so on. You can only participate in the economic game if you overcome all these entry barriers – where the incumbents often determine the judges and regulators – which is an almost hopeless task for small businesses and fledgling entrepreneurs who have a good idea and a great appetite for business but no knowledge of the complexity of those apparently necessary, but largely unnecessary, regulations. Large corporations, however, try to raise these entry barriers even higher because complexity, regulation, and licensing help to sustain their dominant position.

So, although gigantism has a multiplicity of causes, it results primarily from top-down systems. Another important catalyst is excessive corporatism in the Western world and the belief in almost mathematical economic laws. Thousands of students trained in these economic dogmas graduate each year and end up in high-ranking positions. The blind conviction that "free trade is always good for prosperity," for example, has enormous consequences for the climate and our social systems. For decades, increasing and under-regulated free trade, and its social and environmental consequences, went unquestioned. Gross domestic product grew, but today we also see other consequences, which are destroying prosperity.

Government intervention, which Keynes encouraged, also has adverse side effects because it leads to the distortion of competition and sometimes to overstimulation and excessive corporate debt, which result in overcapacity, the phenomenon of "zombie companies," and ultimately sub-optimal economic outcomes, both for the government (competitiveness of its economy) and for the companies (unfair competition). Zombie companies are those that would not survive without government intervention in the form of extensive subsidies or extremely low interest rates. It was, in fact, the European Central Bank (ECB) (which promoted zombification with its low interest rates) that pointed out the danger of zombification in the European economy in May 2021. Nearly one in ten companies would classify as a zombie company, according to the bank.[8]

In addition, the government cannot accurately gauge all the consequences of its policies. Some, such as social consequences, often do not appear until later. Industrial policy is a typical example, where governments too often try to identify "the winners" of the future and make those the focus of their policy. Attracting multinational companies with strong tax incentives has also had unintended consequences for local businesses or has shifted those burdens onto other economic actors. Financial and environmental effects can also remain invisible for a long time. For this reason, economies marked by a high level of government intervention are not sustainable: we witnessed the decline of planned economies in the past, such as those in the former Eastern bloc and in other regions.

Particularly crucial is the realization that purely economic thinking neglects many dimensions and can therefore have a poor social outcome. In other words, we need fewer pure economists and more economists with experience in other branches of the university world: psychology, science, sociology, and law. We also need economists with experience in the real world. Academic economists can learn a great deal from business economists, and vice versa. The disdain with which some academics regard non-academic economists is extremely unfortunate and does not improve policy. Above all, however, we need more economists – academic or not – with philosophical and ethical insight.

Scale Brings Advantages, But the Disadvantages Are Underappreciated

Economists believe in economies of scale – one of the dogmas we discussed earlier. Quite simply, there are advantages that an organization or a company gains when it grows or, for example, takes over another organization. There are obvious efficiency gains in production, the purchase of raw materials, the well-known division of tasks, specialization, and many other areas. Adam Smith himself described this principle, but he also paid attention to the excesses, especially when scale would lead to a lack of competition through monopolies, oligopolies, or cartels. The disadvantages of increasing scale were also identified but were often related to limitations in the supply of raw materials, the size of the market, or a lack of labour. However, in today's economy without real market boundaries, it seems that there are only advantages. The disadvantages in the economic field are indeed limited, but they are to be found in entirely different areas.

Hence it is no surprise that armies of consultants have propagated the benefits of increasing scale. There is a lot of money to be made in the process because mergers and acquisitions are among the most lucrative branches of financial services, and the consultants and specialists have proclaimed this economic axiom far beyond the economic sectors. Like missionaries, they spread the word, introducing it into schools, hospitals, administrations, and all other institutions. Consequently, thinking in terms of scale has become a social phenomenon in recent decades.

Unfortunately there are not only economic disadvantages but also many other harmful consequences of increasing the size of organizations. Perhaps we should just start with the fact that the much-touted benefits are often underwhelming. The resulting economies of scale are usually disappointing. Much literature has been published on "synergies," the hoped-for efficiency gains from merging different entities. Synergies, however, are affected by various factors such as cultural differences, the overestimation of potential, and the loss of clients and key talents, or quite simply because the advisors or managers who are keen on making an acquisition paint a rosier picture in order to push through a deal.

More importantly, the impact on other areas – social, ecological, psychological, and so on – is ignored. Large institutions are impersonal, distant, bureaucratic, and frightening. The question, however, is, When does big become too big? The German philosopher Leopold Kohr (1909–1994) said:

> Wherever something is wrong, something is too big. If the stars in the sky or the atoms of uranium disintegrate in a spontaneous explosion, it is not because their substance has lost its balance. It is because matter has attempted to expand beyond the impassable barriers set to every accumulation. Their mass has become too big. If the human body becomes diseased, it is, as in [the case of] cancer, because a cell, or a group of cells, has begun to outgrow its allotted narrow limits. And if the body of a people becomes diseased with the fever of aggression, brutality, collectivism or massive idiocy, it is not because it has fallen victim to bad leadership or mental derangement. It is because human beings, so charming as individuals or in small aggregations, have been welded into overconcentrated social units such as mobs, [trade] unions, cartels, or great powers.[9]

Kohr's doctrine tends towards anarchism, towards the rejection of any structure, but also contains many elements that can offer solutions today: decentralization, city-states, and the cherishing of the philosophy that small is beautiful.

His pupil Ernst Friedrich Schumacher (1911–1977) sought a somewhat more moderate path and was one of the first to realize that economic growth would have enormous ecological consequences. Schumacher owed his early career to Keynes and upon Keynes's death wrote his obituary for the British newspaper *The Times*. The founder of "small" was thus made big by the father of gigantism. It is also bizarre that he worked for a long time as a lobbyist for the British coal industry, but he ultimately owed his fame to work that is a foundation of environmental awareness in economic thinking. Schumacher would undoubtedly have been pleased with this book, although he would not find my proposed solutions to be radical enough. While I would like to tackle the excesses and adjust the rules of the game to make growth more sustainable and to prevent gigantism, Schumacher would have gone even further and preached more antiglobalism and more extreme localism than that of small countries or city-states. In this way, however, one tends towards the other extreme, trying to impose a kind of utopian society that only a small minority of the population would really want. And people would feel restricted in their freedom or ability to develop their talents. There is the risk that you would end up in a leftist totalitarian system of socialism that had gone too far. Purely socialist systems lead to the curtailment of personal development and freedom and to the stagnation of innovation and productivity. Moreover, they ultimately fail to create enough wealth to continue to finance the (at times excessive) socialist promises. It could be worse because communist ideals are still lurking right around the corner. They are imposed by a minority and impoverish as well as subjugate the population, intellectually and materially.

It is perhaps for this reason that Schumacher's ideas (such as small is beautiful) never really caught on. Finding a balance between left and right, between gigantic and cuddly, between globalism and small-town mentality is a difficult socio-economic exercise. The extremes are clearer and find fervent supporters – sometimes out of pure self-interest, at other times out of intellectual laziness. In order to find the balance, one has to analyze and try to understand the positions of each side and from them distill the best elements. For example, my analysis of schools and hospitals, and the institutionalization of these important services, is partly in line with the Austrian philosopher Ivan Illich (1926–2002). Illich warned long ago that standardization and norms lead to things like pressure to perform in education and pressure to consume in the health-care sector.[10] Yet I do not consider myself by any means to be a progress pessimist who sees technology as a creeping evil. On the contrary, I see technology as part of the solution that will enable us to manage increasingly decentralized systems – not only in information and communications but also increasingly in the energy and logistics sectors. So why not in public services, education, and health care, too?

Returning to the questions "When does something become too big, and does scale have disadvantages?" I posit that there is no single, quantifiable answer. Economists would say in answer to the first question: when an increase in additional output causes an increase in the unit cost of a product. That, however, does not take into account the social, environmental, or not obviously calculable, economic costs. Economists agree that concentration is not good, but unfortunately the mechanisms surrounding its control and regulation have been weakened, especially outside Europe. Organizations should give greater consideration to customer and employee satisfaction, but unfortunately this is measured neither frequently nor consistently, or the dissatisfaction is only noticed when it is too late.

What is also remarkable is that consultants and experts are lining up to praise and defend scale but rarely, if ever, recommend downsizing. Why would that be? The bigger the organization, the more specialization, the more need for specialists, and also the more need for all sorts of managers. This explains the bias: experts thrive on complexity and scale. Small organizations have less demand for their services. That is why it is advisable to always keep the power of the experts in balance with the freedom of the individual. Smaller, more decentralized organizations are closer to the individual and have greater freedom. It is important for individuals to retain their freedom and not be moulded into meek followers by a system and its experts. This does not mean that experts cannot play a constructive role, or that they do not possess valuable knowledge, but it should be understood that on a societal level these experts also have an interest in greater complexity, control, and scale.

Decision makers are likely to call on a board of reliable experts, particularly during crises. In such a situation it is important to take into account sufficient diversity and independence. Experts closely connected to a lobby not only are undesirable but could potentially prove very damaging to the interests of society. In crisis situations it is tempting to give experts considerable decision-making power, but it is precisely at these times that adequate democratic control is also needed. Gigantism did not appear overnight, but it is clear to me that experts played a role in its emergence. With each crisis, new report, new analysis, and subsequent decision, power is drawn upwards, rather than being decentralized.

Keynes was a key expert after the First World War and during and shortly after the Second World War. His theory was regularly revived in the following decades, most notably after the financial crisis of 2008. But his insights are not infallible and they involve new risks in the economic and social field; today's gigantism is one example, but the escalation of deficit spending and the accumulation of deficits and debt also carry risks. Keynes's theories are probably time bound or even misinterpreted today. We remember deficit spending, but we do not, for example, build up buffers in good times, as Keynes recommended. In my opinion, people started over-consuming his economic medicines before the crisis of the 1930s.

The role of experts is crucial during every pivotal moment, when they help determine the policy and can shift it in a certain direction. This was the case after the financial crisis of 2008, when neo-Keynesians such as Paul Krugman came to the fore. Amid the COVID-19 crisis, experts were again brought in, most of whom lauded the role of big government. Among them was Mariana Mazzucato, professor of economics of innovation and public value at University College London. In short, Mazzucato wants to convince us that every great innovation happened with government intervention.[11] However, that depends very much on what you attribute to the government: a course at a university, an order placed with a company on behalf of the army, or the granting of a certain percentage of funding for research and development. The real difference, however, is that great innovations and breakthroughs usually came about through collaboration and the readiness of a few people to take risks and persist. Government is important for creating a stable framework, but belief in big government dampens the creativity and initiative of individuals and organizations.

Another rising star is Stephanie Kelton. She is involved in the development of Modern Monetary Theory (MMT) and is a professor at Stony Brook University, New York. Her theory appeals to left-wing thinkers, but it is not modern and lacks monetary logic. Kelton emphasizes unlimited opportunities for governments with the use of their own currencies to incur debt, make public investments, and achieve full employment.[12] It is "Keynes on steroids." Should we pursue her approach, money will devalue, bubbles will appear, and the confidence to make long-term financial decisions will vanish. Kelton believes in the wisdom of government to restrain its activities, whereas the opposite is true: without clear limits a government will always expand its limits until it implodes. Even Paul Krugman, though a neo-Keynesian, does not consider MMT to be a stable and coherent theory, calling it a mess.[13] The problem with unlimited debt and stretching the role of governments and central banks is that it erodes trust in the system. Building trust takes enormous effort, but it can evaporate in an instant and destabilize the economy for a long time.

Keynesians and neo-Keynesians do not agree on everything, but they share, willingly or unwillingly, a preference for "big" – big corporations and big government. Today they find much support for this approach in politics, the elite, and the media, but other advice that could restore the balance during a crisis is lost as a result. As was the case after the 2008 financial crisis, too little attention is paid to the importance of buffers, safety systems, margins in the system, and the adequate burden sharing of risks. The crisis in Ukraine today reveals the same thing: the West failed to take sufficient account of scenarios and risks, thereby becoming vulnerable to disruptions. As from now, countries and companies will amass more buffers and build in redundancies and safety margins. They will also learn to consider different scenarios, instead of believing that big state can guarantee a blue-sky scenario.

The most important role for economists and policy-makers remains the same as for firefighters: it is not the capacity to extinguish fires efficiently that determines one's success, but one's ability to prevent them. I blame the central bankers and policy-makers, but also the bankers and business leaders. Frequent interventionism has created a sense of irresponsibility. The big hand of government has to step in with solutions when things go wrong – financially, socially, and climatologically. And as the government carries out ever larger bailouts, the risks involved are bigger, never smaller. When Allan Greenspan rescued a USD 4.7 billion "giant leveraged fund" with USD 129 billion in positions, he thought he was pulling off a once-only conjuring trick. During the financial crisis USD 4.7 billion turned out to be a fraction of what systemic banks and other hedge funds had built up. By rescuing them again, central banks themselves have become leveraged funds with huge positions relative to their own assets. The lesson is that big government does not lead to prudence but rather to irresponsibility.

The COVID-19 crisis gave another massive boost to big business and stimulated big government. During the coronavirus pandemic, gigantism was stimulated from all sides. The tech giants watched their business boom through e-commerce, the omnipresent virtual video conferencing, and a myriad of other activities such as cloud services and even games. Small shops, local culture and events, and all manner of in-person contacts and services suffered as a result. Amazon boss Jeff Bezos saw his wealth skyrocket, to the extent that he was able to turn his attention to space, light years away from the worldly problems of the little man. But there were also unprecedented government interventions – first out of necessity to quell the pandemic, but then by rolling out Keynesian measures again and in overdrive. The billions in relaunch and pandemic projects are distributed top-down and are tailored to the largest companies. John Maynard Keynes would approve. Big pharma was the lifesaver, with a plethora of much-needed vaccines, in collaboration with the government, and big pharma fortified its position in the process. The small entrepreneur and the individual were suffocated by rules and COVID-19 setbacks. The crisis in Ukraine, and especially its consequences on energy, food, and defence, will reinforce the call for more government. The demand for more intervention and more government will only increase in the coming years. Sadly, the solutions lie particularly in innovation and in the ingenuity of entrepreneurs and individuals. Scarcity and higher prices breed creativity, which must not be curbed excessively by the removal of incentives such as higher prices. Big government kills any seed of change before it has a chance to germinate.

Keynes cherished the illusion that in moments of crisis the government could intervene with public expenditure or other measures. As a result, however, economic actors are behaving increasingly recklessly because the government will step in if things go wrong. This creates a climate of collective irresponsibility because governments will always shoulder that burden. Consequently the same governments need to intervene with even greater frequency. The evidence bears this out: the balance sheets of central banks are historically high, as are public debts. The margin for intervention is becoming ever narrower, while the necessary intervention is in danger of becoming increasingly massive in order to stabilize or "save" the system. The ultimate consequence of these interventions is that capitalism is eroding from within. It is more and more about government and less and less about market mechanisms and responsible individuals.

The Ultimate and Gigantic "Tragedy of the Commons": Our Climate

Economists have long known the problem of "commons." It occurs when individuals fail to take care of the shared resources for which they are jointly responsible. There are countless examples of these resources. Fish stocks in the oceans are often cited, while examples closer to home include bus shelters, public parks, playing grounds, skate parks, libraries, museums, and freedom of speech. When economists speak of "the tragedy of the commons," they mean that the quality of the commons deteriorates more rapidly than that of private goods. The "common" (common property) was an open field or village green on which, unlike on privately owned, enclosed pastures, anyone could graze their flock. The quality of these commons invariably declined more than that of private land did. If no one feels personally responsible for clean air, pollution, or public goods, it is impossible for the government to guarantee them fully and in perpetuity. The financial system is a public good that deteriorated in the run-up to the 2008 crisis, and today we are experiencing the tragedy of the *climate* commons. Climate challenges have assumed immense proportions because we did not act responsibly and we failed to protect this vital public good.

Can capitalism safeguard common goods? Today's global capitalism has clearly failed to do so. Our air quality, the Amazon rainforest, fish stocks, and all kinds of biodiversity and extraordinary animal species are endangered, and the form of capitalism that was in place could not prevent it (though, for instance, Brazil, China, and Russia cannot be

labelled capitalistic economies). But the solution provided by government regulations is minimal. What works particularly well is to give a
capitalist system the right incentives to reward the careful use, or even
improvement, of the commons. Ronald Coase, who won the Nobel Prize
in 1991, developed this theory in 1960 in his article "The Problem of
Social Cost." The negative consequences, also known as negative externalities, of the use of public goods can be limited and even eliminated
by allowing the private parties to negotiate the price of those goods.
This is the keystone of emissions trading (known as ETS in Europe). The
government determines the volume of carbon dioxide (CO_2) that can
be emitted in a given year and grants "allowances," whose price is determined by the market. Companies that cannot reduce their emissions
have to buy allowances from companies that can. One example is Tesla,
which receives hundreds of millions of dollars from car manufacturers
who build cars that still emit CO_2. The car makers themselves will
become guardians of this system and, if they do not make deals, can do so
more efficiently than the government can. As yet, there is no worldwide
CO_2 emission system, but if one were introduced, it could significantly
accelerate the reduction of CO_2. If logistics flows were to take people
and the environment into account, the trend towards ever-larger ships,
ports, and other connected activities would be curtailed.

So why has capitalism failed to rectify climate derailment? A hundred
or so giants are responsible for over 70 per cent of greenhouse gas emissions.[14] What is often forgotten is that most are state-owned corporations,
and many are well-known private companies, particularly in the energy
sector. These large private companies are highly organized, with excellent
government contacts, extensive lobbying, and large financial resources
to bring to bear on decisions. This lobbying ensured that the Paris
Agreement went no further and, for instance, introduced a global CO_2
tax. At meetings like those of the World Economic Forum in Davos
considerable lip service is paid to the climate, but tough measures are
rarely advocated, and large polluters are not excluded from participation
in the conference. So capitalism has not failed; to the contrary, the lack
of capitalism is the cause – the fake capitalism of big companies, lobbies,
and rent-seekers.

There has been a long and collective irresponsibility in the climate
debacle on the part of governments and private players alike, and
now that the process is in danger of coming off the rails, people are

counting on powerful governments to solve the problem. Just as the responsibility is collective, the solution will also be collective: encouraging the ingenuity of the best scientists, guiding self-interest towards a carbon-free economy, and imposing fines on non-compliant countries and companies or excluding them from world trade. The system will not function smoothly unless there are real economic consequences.

Capitalism is the best system for organizing our economy – but not in its present form. It is precisely this derivative current form that lies at the basis of gigantism. To save capitalism and eradicate fake capitalism we will have to take more profound measures: first of all in the area of cartels, but that is just a start. Crony capitalism also needs to be recognized and stopped, both regionally and internationally. It will not be easy to implement these measures globally, however, and the problems in the major economic blocs are different. The G-7 or G-20 nations should put this on the agenda as a matter of urgency, as a condition for free trade agreements. We see the first signs of this condition with the Organisation for Economic Co-operation and Development's initiative of a global minimum corporate tax, as designed by its director Pascal Saint-Amans.

The Continent is already quite successful at imposing a growth diet on its regional champions. Europe is not quick to allow megamergers – a strong example being set by executive vice-president and commissioner for competition Margrethe Vestager – sometimes because of old nationalistic interests but also because of concentration and the possible impact on innovation and diversity. China and the United States are less aware of the importance of doing so and let their giants thrive. They continue to believe firmly in the national interest of economic giants and the role these large corporations play in economic imperialism. Although it is clear that the Chinese and American economies are gradually beginning to suffer from gigantism, it will take some time before the pendulum swings in the opposite direction. Yet, without international agreements the economic superpowers will not arrive at the same conclusion.

If we want to curb gigantism, we must change the rules of globalization. Social and ecological costs play too small a role in global economic choices. If economic incentives are all that count in optimizing production, then people and the environment will suffer. I have already pointed out the importance of a global CO_2 tax on international logistical movements. Such a tax would change the economic game entirely. Local production would become possible again, and many international logistics movements would cease to make economic sense. Likewise, more human rights could be factored into international trade, as happened in the past with child labour. The raising of consumer awareness can also play a role; buyers do not always know where their goods come from and, if they are better informed, they will make different choices. In financial markets we see a growing role for environmental, social, and governance (ESG) investments, which divert money flows to companies that have greater respect for these rules. Although there is a great deal of greenwashing (companies portraying themselves as more environmentally responsible than they are), the impact is unmistakable. In the end, fully in line with Adam Smith's approach, companies prefer to be counted among the "good" by the "impartial spectator." When steered in the direction of the common good, self-interest – of consumers and businesses – is a powerful engine of economic activity.

Economics is a game played by millions of people worldwide. The rules of play and how subtle they may be determine the direction in which the game moves, round after round. The slightest alteration to the rules has enormous consequences for the outcome of the game and for how people play. For this reason game-makers are wary of cheating and of interpreting the rules flexibly. To understand how gigantism comes about, one need only invite a few friends or family members to play Monopoly. You, dear reader, may play the bank.

Cheating at Monopoly Turns into Gigantism

The rules of Monopoly are simple. For example, if someone ends up on an expensive street and cannot pay the rent (and cannot take an additional mortgage on his streets), the game is over for him. But most players have gradually discovered a convenient trick for getting around this: the bank gives everyone the same banknote, allowing the bankrupt player to continue. That simple hack, however, changes the whole game. Without the intervention of the bank, it pays to not take too much risk and to keep enough cash on hand, hence playing it prudently. With the intervention of the bank, it pays to take a lot of risk (buying many streets, rushing to place houses or hotels) because your possible return increases enormously. If you know you will be bailed out by the bank, taking on more risk than other players do will guarantee you to win the

GAME OVER

The first player who goes bankrupt withdraws, just like in the normal game.

But as soon as a second player goes bankrupt, the game is over.

The bankrupt player gives the creditor (the bank or another player) everything he owns, including houses, hotels, and other properties.

Now the remaining players add up the value of their possessions:

1 cash money;
2 the prices indicated on the board for utilities or stations they own;
3 half the price indicated on the board for mortgaged property;
4 the purchase price of the houses they own; and
5 the purchase price of the hotels they own (hotel = the price of four houses).

The richest player wins the game!

Figure 1.1   Original rules of Monopoly

Source: Lizzie Magie, Charles Darrow, and Hasbro Publishers.

game. Players who would otherwise play more cautiously immediately change their approach and take far greater risks. Therefore, the attitude of the banker changes prudent buyers into speculators.

When the bank starts distributing money, other effects swiftly occur: the supply of houses and hotels is exhausted, and some players accrue so much money that they can build a second or third hotel. This adjustment of the rules is accepted by a large number of Monopoly players (who apparently interpret the rules rather freely). The player who takes the most risk amasses streets and hotels; the cautious player is relegated to the sidelines and watches as arrears increase over time.

The intervention of the bank now has two effects: the player who takes the most risk will win, whereas in the original game there was a trade-off between risk and return. Moreover, the most reckless player will gradually dominate all the streets with even more hotels. The original rules compelled players to be circumspect; the new rules allow the biggest speculator to win. This highlights another effect of the bank's intervention: over-investment and asset inflation (excessively high prices). Eventually the game of Monopoly will end because it no longer makes sense to play: the supply of money is exhausted, as are the hotels. The players do not see the fun of the game anymore and stop playing.

Central banks in today's global economy are the Monopoly bank, you are the cautious player, and the giants are aware that the game is played differently.

2

GIGANTISM?

In the previous chapter I outlined today's world economy and touched on what the phenomenon of gigantism entails. Naturally, it is only fitting to offer a clear, detailed definition of this new economic concept.

Gigantism has, until now, been a rather curious term to use in relation to economics. The concept is taken from biology and refers to flora and fauna that suffer from excessive growth. The condition is also known by other names, such as macrosomia, hypersomia, and acromegaly – none of which struck me as a catchy title for a book. They sound bleak, even to economists who practise the dismal science. All these terms refer to the same thing: the abnormal growth in size or stature of a body caused by an overproduction of growth hormone. Typically, organisms can grow too large through excessive stimuli, through an overproduction of growth hormone.

A condition that has an impact on living beings can also affect organizations: some companies, institutions, non-governmental organizations (NGOs), international organizations, and football clubs also achieve abnormal growth and become "giants." This is not a healthy state of affairs for the economy, which is why we can safely use the term *economic disease*. It is an unbalanced situation, a state of economic disorder that, to some degree, is contagious and can contaminate other sectors and activities. Everything must eventually be able to scale up to the size of the giants, as we witnessed overnight when, in 2021, the Suez Canal proved too small for the megavessel *Ever Given*. We suddenly realized just how vulnerable we were when the 200,000 tonne container ship blocked the vital waterway for six days, and more than four hundred other megaships were trapped in the resulting logjam. The entire international logistics system went into cardiac arrest, and factories and consumers suddenly realized how connected they were to far-flung supply points. Eventually the ship was refloated, and the Suez Canal authorities initiated plans to expand the canal.

Gigantism is both contagious and economically unhealthy, as the analysis will show, and therefore must be treated or, better still, prevented. In humans, gigantism is rare. Economically, everyone feels it has become a dominant factor. What has become evident instinctively and through incidents such as the *Ever Given*, however, deserves a brief introductory sketch. Do large organizations, oversized corporations, and outsized economic entities pose a problem? Or is it a figment of our imagination? And is this not the way it has always been?

Diagnosing economic gigantism is far from simple. Establishing gigantism objectively is best done in three ways.

First, one can determine abnormal size and compare it with historical observations. Do we see gigantic companies and organizations today in a format and with a frequency that we did not see before? Second, gigantism is also about behaviours that indicate the excesses of companies that have grown too large in their sector or activity. Economists look for excessively high margins or excessive profits in certain sectors or companies. Third, it is also about concentration. In other words, we can pinpoint three traits: excessive size, concentration, and excessive profit margins (when it comes to private companies) are indicators of gigantism. If we can identify this pathology, we know irrefutably that the disease is present.

Next, we can refine the diagnosis, identify the symptoms, and consider ways of curing this economic disease.

Size Matters

It is not difficult to find figures that show that large companies are taking an ever-increasing share of our economy. All countries and all sectors are affected. In the United States the share of added value created by the two hundred largest companies increased from 30 to almost 45 per cent in the post-war period. The greatest increase occurred up until 1975, but in the last two decades the upward trend has resumed. According to McKinsey & Company, six hundred companies take 80 per cent of the economic profits generated worldwide.[1]

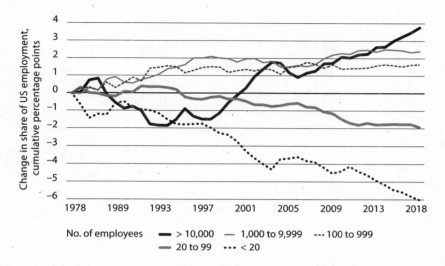

Figure 2.1   Big business is getting bigger: Evolution of the size of companies in the United States

Source: Author's calculations based on US Census Bureau data, https://www.census.gov/programs-surveys/susb/data/tables.2018.html; Leonhardt, "The Charts."

The New York Times investigated the size of US companies and came to the same conclusion. "Getting bigger" is a trend among companies (see figure 2.1). The number of large groups is constantly growing, whether measured by market capitalization,[2] as a proportion of the added value, or by the number of employees they employ. I will amply demonstrate that these companies want to become bigger because they believe it gives them a crucial advantage: being big leads to greater power, which ultimately leads to bigger profits. As the competitors grow, competing companies will pursue the same goal: to increase in size. It is an endless cycle, with everyone chasing each other's tail.

This does not happen without a fight. Politicians occasionally point out the dangers. Ro Khanna, a Democrat congressman from Silicon Valley, California, drew attention to them in a 2018 speech: "One of the things that people in this country are rebelling against is large, growing institutions. People feel that they are losing control of their own destiny."[3] This is just one of the consequences of gigantism that will be discussed in detail in the following chapters. First, let us take a closer look at the disease and not dwell too much on the symptoms and the patients who complain about it.

Table 2.1   Largest listed technology companies in the world, as of 31 January 2023

	Market capitalization (USD billions)
Baidu	38
Alibaba	313
Tencent	507
Total BAT	858
Apple	2,310
Amazon	1,040
Facebook/META	398
Netflix	160
Alphabet (Google)	1,300
Total FAANG	5,208
Microsoft	1,850
Oracle	240
Intel	116
Broadcom	247
Cisco	199
NVIDIA	501
IBM	121
NASDAQ 100	14,111
NASDAQ Composite	18,848
S&P 500	34,063

Source: Bloomberg.

The most striking feature of table 2.1 is the increase in the market capitalization of large corporations, in other words, the total value of the shares of a company according to their prices. The American tech companies Apple, Google, and Microsoft flirt with and largely exceed the limit of USD 1,000 billion market capitalization. Even if 30 per cent is accrued or evaporates on the stock exchange, it does little to change the situation: as megacorporations they continue to dominate the economy, even on a global scale. Tech companies are not the only corporate giants; in terms of market capitalization, number of employees, balance sheets, and turnover, pharmaceutical groups and banks are also gigantic.

Table 2.2   Size of US listed companies, inflation adjusted at September 2007

1917 Assets (USD billions)	1967 Assets (USD billions)	2022 Assets (USD billions)
U.S. Steel 46 Steel	International Business Machines 259 Technology	Apple 1,680 Technology
American Telephone & Telegraph 14 Telecom	American Telephone & Telegraph 2001 Telecom	Microsoft 1,300 Technology
Standard Oil of N.J. 11 Oil & Gas	Eastman Kodak 177 Film	Alphabet (Google) 882 Technology
Bethlehem Steel 7 Steel	General Motors 171 Automotive	Amazon 726 Retail/Technology
Armour & Co. 6 Food	Standard Oil of N.J. 107 Oil & Gas	Berkshire Hathaway 4825 Holding
Swift & Co. 6 Food	Texaco 82 Oil & Gas	Tesla 430 Automotive
International Harvester 5 Machinery	Sears, Roebuck 65 Retail	UnitedHealth 344 Health & Insurance
E.I. Du Pont de Nemours 5 Chemistry	General Electric 64 Conglomerate	Exxon Mobil 331 Oil & Energy
Midvale Steel & Ordnance 5 Steel	Polaroid 58 Film	Johnson & Johnson 312 Pharma
U.S. Rubber 5 Rubber	Gulf Oil 58 Oil & Gas	Visa 305 Financial Services

Sources: "A Century of America's Top 10 Companies, in One Chart," howmuch.net/articles/
100-years-of-americas-top-10-companies; forbes.com.

Table 2.2 shows that, converted to present dollar values, the size of US businesses today is indeed exceptional.[4] And we should not focus solely on the United States; China's largest companies also rank among the global titans.

Table 2.3   Largest listed companies in Europe,* November 2022

Top 10	Country	Market capitalization (EUR billions, rounded)
LVMH	France	367
Nestlé	Switzerland	316
Roche	Switzerland	285
Novo Nordisk	Denmark	251
ASML	Netherlands	229
Shell	United Kingdom	202
Astrazeneca	United Kingdom	196
L'Oréal	France	192
Accenture	Ireland	183
Novartis	Switzerland	181
Total		2,723

* European Union, United Kingdom, and Switzerland

Source: MSCI Inc.

In 2019 the world's stock exchanges were dominated by technology companies. The top twenty were neatly divided between the United States and China, with the very largest companies being American and the rest a mix. It means that the Asian superpower has almost the same number of tech giants as the United States has. For every Amazon you will find an Alibaba, for every Apple a Xiaomi.

The market capitalization of Alibaba Group and Tencent Holdings is comparable to that of their American counterparts. The six largest American tech companies are as big as the next ninety-four American technology companies combined. That is impressive in terms of size but also indicates a particularly high level of concentration (see table 2.1).

The size of businesses in Europe is now significantly smaller than the size of those in other regions (see table 2.3). The three largest European companies together – the food group Nestlé, the oil and gas company Royal Dutch Shell, and the pharmaceutical giant Roche – are smaller than Apple, the largest US company measured by market capitalization. It is also striking that five of the ten largest European companies come from outside the euro area, and that there is only one tech company (ASML Holding) in the top ten, though there are oil multinationals and banks. All of this clearly shows that Europe is still mired in the old sectors and largely missed in the new economy.

Stock markets are not the only yardstick for determining size. In Europe there are large groups that dominate a sector but are not listed on the stock exchange, such as the Swedish home furnishings store Ikea or the French sports retail chain Decathlon SA. This is also the case in China, where the smart-phone manufacturer Huawei Technologies is not listed on the stock exchange. In addition, promising European companies are often prey for American or Chinese giants, even before they have a chance to become very large, such as the hotel website Booking.com or the Finnish game developer Supercell Oy. The Swedish streaming platform Spotify is still an exception, but that can soon change.

There is another important reason that large corporations are less prevalent in Europe than in the United States: the antitrust policy in Europe is much stricter than that on the other side of the Atlantic. It is also more difficult to find European champions who can compete with top American players because the antitrust policy begins at the national level. For example, fifteen years ago Sweden blocked the merger of Scania AB and the Volvo Group even though the merged company would not have dominated the truck market at the European level. In 2019 the EU blocked the merger of train manufacturers Alstom SA and Siemens AG. The European Commission is cracking down on European companies but fails to impose the same rules on American companies. Consequently we have dwarf companies in large sectors. There are exceptions, and it is no coincidence that they are to be found in market segments with powerful lobbying machines: the financial sector and the pharmaceutical sector.

Europe excels at governmental gigantism, however. German chancellor Angela Merkel once stated: "While Europe today accounts for only seven per cent of the world's population, we produce around twenty-five per cent of the world's gross domestic product and finance fifty per cent of global social spending. We will therefore have to work very hard to maintain our prosperity and way of life."[5] The European governments have themselves become the giants, with extensive and generalized public spending, huge funds for agriculture, regional development – or, soon, CO_2 reduction investments. This creates a completely different economic dynamic, one in which the giants are not the companies or their chief executive officers (CEOs) but are the European institutions and the European political leaders alongside a whole host of national administrations and institutions, which causes a great deal of red tape.

Table 2.4   Largest companies in China, November 2022

Ranking	Company	Market capitalization (USD billions)	Sector	Type
1	Tencent	329	Technology	Public, state-owned enterprise
2	Kweichow Moutai	270	Food & Beverages	Public, state-owned enterprise
3	ICBC	202	Banking	State-owned enterprise
4	Alibaba	187	Technology	Public, state-owned enterprise
5	China Construction Bank	148	Banking	Public, state-owned enterprise
6	China Mobile	142	Telecom	Public, state-owned enterprise
7	CATL	138	Batteries	Public
8	Agricultural Bank of China	135	Banking	Public, state-owned enterprise
9	Meituan	128	Technology/Retail	Public
10	PetroChina	124	Oil	Public, state-owned enterprise

Source: *Fortune*, https://fortune.com/global500/2020/search/?fg500_country=China.

In China there are huge companies whose size is difficult to measure because they are often state owned: for example, large banks and energy corporations (see table 2.4). Listed technology companies do not appear in this case. These giants are usually controlled by the government. The problem is that they take over private companies in other parts of the world without having to comply with the same rules. State-owned Chinese companies can buy up competitors in Europe in sectors where state aid is explicitly prohibited. This leads to distortions of competition.

The Dutch East India Company (Vereenigde Oost-Indische Compagnie, or VOC), which operated from 1602 to 1800, would have had a market value of approximately USD 8,000 billion in today's dollars (see figure 2.2). As of the end of 2022, this was as much as the fifteen largest US technology companies together. However, using a historical comparison to frame the size of companies is not easy. Stock markets were not yet as developed as they are today, statistics were not accurately kept, states and companies were more interwoven, and there is a large margin of error if you convert century-old values into today's euros and dollars. The VOC was the first real joint-stock company with freely

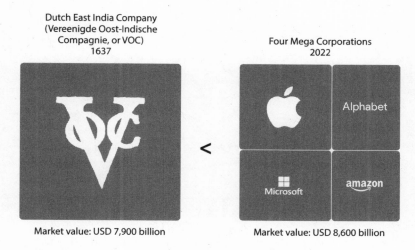

Market value: USD 7,900 billion   Market value: USD 8,600 billion

Figure 2.2   World's largest company collapsed due to mismanagement: Size of companies in historical perspective

Source: VOC value – Barry Ritholtz, https://www.visualcapitalist.com/most-valuable-companies-all-time/; value of current companies recalculated by author.

tradable shares. The trading company had its own army and employed nearly 30,000 people at its peak. Corruption and mismanagement were the company's undoing.

The American economist and opinion maker Barry Ritholtz brought together data on the size of other gigantic companies from the distant and not-so-distant past.[6]

- Saudi Aramco, the state oil company of Saudi Arabia, had a theoretical value of USD 4,100 billion (converted to today's dollars) in 2010, according to calculations by Professor Sheridan Titman of the University of Texas.
- PetroChina, the state-owned Chinese company active in the energy sector, had a market value of USD 1,400 billion in today's terms in 2007.
- Standard Oil, the oil concern of the legendary John D. Rockefeller, had a market value of USD 1,000 billion in 1900, just before losing its monopoly. That is about the same size as a series of tech companies today.
- Microsoft had already reached a peak value of USD 900 billion in 1999, the year in which the dot-com bubble was about to burst. Today its market value is USD 2,000 billion.

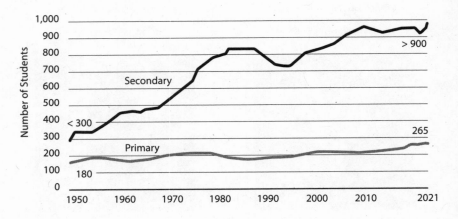

Figure 2.3   Schools give lessons in megalomania: Average school size in the United Kingdom, 1950–2021

The size of schools is on a long upward trend.

Source: House of Commons Library, social indicator 2625, 2017, updated with Education and Training Statistics, 2011–21, Department for Education.

Gigantism does not only affect the corporate entities. In recent decades, other sectors, such as education, health care, and administration, have grown exponentially. Although fewer statistics are available, academics agree that entities in these sectors are following the gigantism trend.

In the United Kingdom, secondary schools have swollen from an average of 300 pupils per school in 1950 to almost 1,000 pupils per entity in 2016. In the United States, the number of colossal schools doubled between the years 2000 and 2016. The vast majority of schools are still small, but the small ones still attract only a minor share of pupils today. The evolution of the scale of education looks spectacular: small schools are disappearing, and the number of medium-sized and especially very large schools is increasing. This phenomenon can be observed in all Western countries. Economists are the main driving force: the advantages of scale are easy to explain, while the advantages of small schools are less easy to measure.

The advantages of small schools are mainly of a social, rather than an economic, nature. Larger entities afford the advantage of offering a greater choice of specialisms or of sharing the best educators on a broader scale. Later in this book, we will see that large schools also present enormous disadvantages, such as higher rates of violence, bullying, and loneliness. These negative factors are much more difficult to measure. The economic adage "larger is more efficient" sounds more appealing and has dominated policy in recent decades.

It is difficult to analyze increases in scale in government services such as the police, fire brigade, or cultural organizations, but in health care, for example, it is very well documented. Italian researchers argue that general hospitals worldwide are becoming increasingly larger and more complex.[7] This obviously offers advantages because small hospitals cannot have all the expertise and cannot keep up with all the technology that modern medicine requires today. However, the same increase in scale does have consequences for the patients, who find themselves in a more industrial environment compared to that of the smaller, less threatening hospitals of the past. The patient trades a potential technological improvement for a potentially less personal, familiar environment. Here too, sizing up is largely stimulated by economic thinking. What we call *economies of scale* is a strong argument for optimizing purely economic efficiency in the health-care sector. Italian research on the phenomenon of economies of scale in the industry discovered that policy-makers are under great pressure to increase concentration in health care and to promote mergers of health-care institutions. This pressure stems from a belief that larger health-care institutions result in lower average costs and better clinical outcomes. In this context, calculating scale efficiency is crucial to achieving optimal size.

Economic criteria are much easier to measure and more widely available than broader qualitative and socio-economic indicators, such as patient confidence and happiness, the involvement of medical staff, and the overall satisfaction of all concerned. These factors are not often measured. If statistics exist at all, they are – unlike purely economic figures – difficult to compare with data from other countries or other entities.

Italian researchers combed the literature and concluded that there was a significant increase in publications indicating economies of scale in health-care institutions. The theme of *scaling up* proved to dominate the debate, especially in recent decades, both in pure business and economics journals and in publications on health care (see table 2.5). The words *returns to scale* (scale revenues) and *economies of scale* (scale

Table 2.5   Gigantism in the hospital sector, a contagious disease: Articles on economies of scale in hospitals

Publication	1969–1989	1990–2000	2001–2014
Business journals and economic magazines	0	9	16
Health-care journals	4	7	34
Medical journals	1	3	8
Management magazines and scientific periodicals	3	6	14
Total	8	25	72

There were almost three times as many articles on economies of scale in 2001–14 than in the decade before the dawn of the millennium.

Source: Giancotti, Guglielmo, and Mauro, "Efficiency and Optimal Size of Hospitals."

advantages) were used three times more than they were before the end of the millennium. In such a culture, in which management becomes more important than patient focus, it should come as no surprise that gigantic health-care institutions are springing up all over the world.

International institutions have also grown larger in recent years. Thirty years ago NGOs were mostly small entities but have since developed into multinationals. There are many examples. Doctors Without Borders, founded in 1971, had more than 45,000 employees in 2022 and a budget of USD 2 billion. The environmental organization Greenpeace was founded in the same year as a small-scale Canadian initiative and today operates worldwide with almost 50,000 volunteers and a budget of USD 300 million. Founded in 1942, the aid organization Oxfam now operates in over a hundred countries. The NGO has more than 1,200 shops worldwide, with a strong presence in the United Kingdom. It has a budget of USD 1 billion. NGOs have thus followed the same path as other multinational organizations and now have specialized management functions – from finance to human resources – to organize their charitable efforts.

Economies of scale and continuous expansion are also a feature of international partnerships. The EU was created in 1951 with six founding countries when it was still called the European Coal and Steel Community (ECSC). The Treaty of Rome and the European Economic Community (EEC) followed in 1957. Several countries joined later, and today the EU has twenty-seven member states. After Brexit, the EU shrank for the first time, perhaps indicating that gigantism has its limitations. The euro area, which is part of the EU, underwent a similar expansion. Originally a group of eleven countries in 1998, the euro area now comprises nineteen countries, and new candidates are still waiting. It is particularly difficult to have a common currency in a heterogeneous economic zone that extends from Finland to Greece. This has been demonstrated repeatedly, for example, with the Latin monetary union, a nineteenth-century version of the euro area.[8] Its founding members were Belgium, France, Italy, and Switzerland; shortly afterwards, Spain and Greece joined, and in 1889 Romania, Bulgaria, Serbia, San Marino, and Venezuela followed. The urge to expand even before stable convergence had been achieved proved too strong, even then. The problems began when, among other things, Greece did not keep to the agreements. Later, the currency union exploded because banknotes were printed to fund the First World War. Despite these historical lessons and the tensions subsequent to the 2008 financial crisis, the euro area will, by and large, continue to expand. In principle, seven more member states will be obligated to introduce the euro. Among them is Sweden, which should have adopted the single currency long ago but has always resisted.

The euro is modelled on the dollar and seeks to match or even surpass the US currency as a reserve currency. It is strange that the euro area does not prioritize stability before pursuing further enlargement. After all, during the financial crisis it became evident that the euro area was far from robust. This is demonstrated time and time again in Italy, where the governing parties repeatedly threaten to leave the euro area. Today, the Greek crisis, which almost caused the explosion of the euro area in 2011, is in a sort of quarantine, but far from being resolved. Like a dormant volcano, it can erupt at any time.

International events also have an irrepressible drive to grow in all dimensions. The first modern Olympic Games dates back to 1896: fourteen countries took part, with 241 athletes in forty-three disciplines. At the Summer Olympics in Rio de Janeiro, Brazil, almost 12,000 athletes from around two hundred countries were represented. This growth goes hand in hand with globalization. But there is more. The proliferation of competitions is another phenomenon: the increasing number of countries competed for medals in more than three hundred sports. Only the largest countries, with the help of the biggest multinational sponsors, can organize Olympic Games on such a scale. The allocation always takes

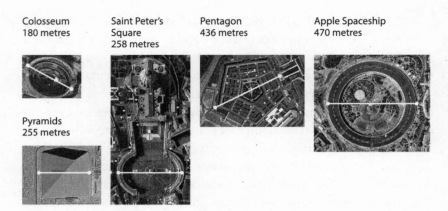

Colosseum
180 metres

Saint Peter's
Square
258 metres

Pentagon
436 metres

Apple Spaceship
470 metres

Pyramids
255 metres

Figure 2.4   Can we supersize this? Gigantism in buildings

Source: Data based on Google Maps.

place behind a veil of corruption and international intrigue. Unfortunately, precious little remains of the original spirit – "Participation is
more important than winning." Today it is about considerable money
and prestige for the organizing cities and countries and the participating
athletes. Some athletes show little respect for the Olympic value of fair
play. Perhaps the Olympic Games would be purer, and closer to the
original spirit, if they were scaled down. However, the International
Olympic Committee seems disinclined to do so. More likely, the event
will have to buckle under its own weight before a reverse movement of
"less is more" can take hold.

The Eurovision Song Contest is another fine example of an event that
is constantly expanding and, with this, losing its identity. In 1956, seven
countries started a song festival: Belgium, France, Italy, Luxembourg,
the Netherlands, the Federal Republic of Germany, and Switzerland.
Ten countries were invited, but Denmark and Austria were too late with
their submissions, and the United Kingdom did not want to participate because it had already organized the Festival of British Popular
Songs – Brexit *avant la lettre*, as it were. In 2019, forty-two countries
participated, including Australia and Israel. Consequently, little remains
of the original song festival, and now cartels are formed to determine
the winner. Everyone's tastes are different, of course, but it is certain
that most of the songs are better off remaining unheard. A new ABBA
or France Gall is rarely discovered.

People have been fascinated by gigantism since ancient times. The Greek and Roman empires were enormous, and with that came prodigious feats of engineering. Such grand creations gave people a sense of power, of being closer to God, of being invincible. Yet compared to modern-day constructions, the pyramids of Egypt or the Colosseum of ancient Rome were small structures (see figure 2.4). The Burj Khalifa in Dubai, the United Arab Emirates, is still the tallest building in the world. But soon the Jeddah Tower in neighbouring Saudi Arabia will outstrip it. The Jeddah Tower, which will take at least four years to complete, will be just over a kilometre high. The pyramid of Cheops, which was also built in a desert – but in Egypt – was only 147 metres high and took twenty years of hard labour to build.

We build increasingly outrageous things, bigger, more impressive, more challenging. It is not only our buildings that grow, but also our machines and vehicles. The Airbus A380 holds 835 passengers, and the 1970s Boeing 747 accommodated 416 passengers – half that. The largest container ship in the world is the OOCL *Hong Kong*: it is 400 metres long and 59 metres wide and can carry 21,400 containers with a total weight of 200,000 tons. The *Titanic* was only 269 metres long and 28 metres wide and weighed 46,000 tons.

Big stimulates bigger: if you make big things, you need big machines. If you use more and more raw materials, larger and larger production sites are required. The biggest ships require bigger dry docks, bigger locks, and bigger ports. When *Ever Given* blocked the Suez Canal, the Dutch economist Mathijs Bouman wrote "that even bigger, even cheaper, even more efficient may be pointless. The tide is turning."[9] Megaships cause port congestion. Everything arrives at the same time and has to leave at the same time, so trucks crowd the roads, and trains cannot cope with the volume of containers. Bouman referred to Marc Levinson, author of the prize-winning book *The Box*, about the rise of containers. Levinson thinks that the peak load caused by the docking of large container ships is inefficient, as they spend longer in port, and transport times have lengthened. Even before *Ever Given* ran aground and blocked the waterway, Levinson wrote that he believed the era of ever-larger container vessels was over.[10] A similar fate befell the Airbus A380. Orders began falling sharply in 2014, and the very last plane to be built left the Toulouse factory on 17 March 2021 for the airline Emirates. Mathijs Bouman suggested that I include a photograph of the stranded *Ever Given* in an updated edition of *Capitalism XXL*.

Likewise, there is a considerable number of gigantic machines. Big Bertha was an immense cannon used by the German army in the First World War. Big Bertha is also the nickname for a huge drill that cost USD 80 million and is used to dig tunnels. The name Bertha actually comes not from the German cannon but from the first female mayor of Seattle, in the United States, where the drill head dug its first three kilometres of tunnel. That Mario Draghi used the name Big Bertha for his "Whatever it takes" intervention is no coincidence. Another example, Bagger 293, is a huge digging machine that was built in Germany in 1995 and requires five people to operate it. Used in German lignite mines, it weighs 14,200 tons and needs a 16.5 megawatt motor. Its dimensions are hard to imagine: 225 metres long and 96 metres high. The machine can mine 219,000 tons of coal per day, with a maximum speed of 28 km per hour. The latter is a completely superfluous piece of trivia because no one would ever dream of taking it out for a spin. Without our ever-increasing appetite for raw materials, such machines would never have been developed. They show that we live in an age of gigantism, in which machines subjugate and nullify humankind.

Unhealthy Concentration in Many Sectors

Size is the most visible sign of gigantism, but this should not blind us; there is far more at play than meets the eye. Concentration indicates gigantism in domains that do not necessarily stand out for their size. For example, monopolies and oligopolies point to unhealthy situations in the economy, where one or a limited number of companies dominate by occupying too large a position. An activity can become too big in a niche market, a giant in a niche market, a dwarf in the total market. In other words, something can become gigantic in a niche market and hence overpower the behaviour of the entire sector.

As it is not easy to measure size, we must look for indirect criteria. Concentration can be an accurate, indirect indicator of unbalanced growth. Concentration means that a few very large players dominate an entire activity and push the smaller ones aside. But how should it be measured? Economists disagree on the objective ways to measure concentration and the size of companies. In the past, employment may have been a good indicator, but in a technological era, a company can become dominant in its sector without having a conspicuously large workforce.

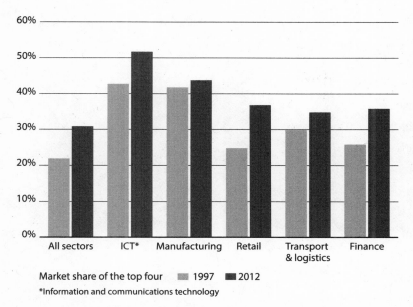

Figure 2.5   Concentration increases in all sectors: Top four companies in different sectors (United States)

Source: US Census Bureau, 1992–2012.

Added value is another possible yardstick. Unfortunately the only sector for which there are sufficiently long-time series to determine company size by this measure is manufacturing. As we know, the importance of manufacturing has declined sharply, which has led us to measure less relevant companies in recent decades.

Another method is to look at the concentration of profits. In the United States one can take the profit evolution of Fortune 500 companies (the 500 largest companies). This shows that they consistently account for just over half of the total US corporate profits. Such raw calculations are, however, not convincing.

Concentration is an economic disease with serious social consequences and is such a crucial symptom of gigantism that I will devote a full chapter to it. The Champions League effect indicates an unhealthy concentration of players occupying a position that makes genuine competition virtually impossible. Barriers to entry are becoming higher all the time, so that newcomers become prey faster than they can achieve champion level.

Researchers have dug deeper and concluded that, in the past two decades in the United States, 75 per cent of sectors were subject to increased concentration. They also observed that, in precisely those

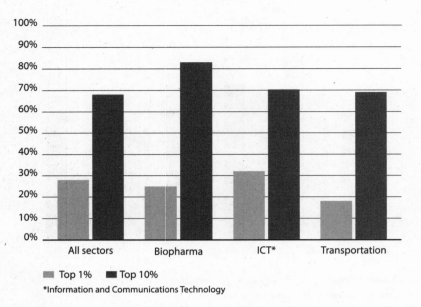

Figure 2.6   A handful of companies account for almost all R&D expenditure:
Concentration of research and development in different sectors

Source: Bruegel, https://www.bruegel.org/sites/default/files/wp-content/uploads/2018/04/
PC-06_2018-110418.pdf; EU Industrial R&D Investment Scoreboard, https://iri.jrc.ec.europa.
eu/scoreboard/2020-eu-industrial-rd-investment-scoreboard#dialog-node-5706.

sectors that experienced the greatest increase in concentration, there
were higher profit margins and lucrative mergers and takeovers. At
the same time, they found no significant improvement in operational
efficiency, indicating that increased market power is an important
source of profitability. They concluded that there is clear evidence that
concentration has increased (see also figure 2.5) and that this has led
to less competition.[11]

Research and development are the basis for future competitiveness.
Expenditure on R&D gives an indication of the future balance of power.
Recent research by the Brussels think tank Bruegel and by Professor
Reinhilde Veugelers shows an extreme concentration in R&D expenditure. One per cent of companies worldwide accounts for a quarter of
such spending. Ten per cent of the world's corporations are responsible for almost three quarters of the total R&D expenditure. There is
a particularly high concentration in biopharma and information and
communication technology (ICT), as well as in the automotive sector

(see figure 2.6). This means that the large companies will try to maintain their lead with enormous R&D budgets. The successful smaller players who stand out from the crowd sooner or later become easy prey for their takeover departments.[12]

Once again, concentration seems less prevalent in Europe, just as, in terms of size, the Continent produced fewer large companies. Once again, research shows that there is less concentration in the European sectors.[13] If anything, it seems that concentration is decreasing in Europe, a trend that researchers attribute to stronger deregulation and stricter antitrust action in the EU.

Higher Profits and Lower Wages in the Economy

This brings us neatly to the third aspect of gigantism: size leading to concentration. Such concentration results in reduced competition, which in turn causes higher profits and margins and lower wages and salaries. The only exception is in the case of the large corporations themselves, which can pay higher than average wages. The International Monetary Fund (IMF) has calculated from the markups – a way of calculating profit margins – that the power of the largest companies has increased enormously since 1980.[14] These calculations show that the largest companies are much more successful at increasing their profit margins than the rest of the business world is. The IMF sees this as evidence that the dominance of these firms has increased. The IMF's conclusions are valid for all the Western industrialized regions and not just the United States (see figure 2.7).

It is striking that the IMF has yet to observe this phenomenon of increased margins and market power in emerging markets, which indicates that it is typical of developed economies – such as Europe, the United States, and Japan. The IMF study also shows how the effect has accelerated in recent years, which could indicate that the consequences of gigantism have shifted into a higher gear.

Another important effect that economists have observed is that globalization not only favours superstar companies but also reduces, and will continue to reduce, the share of labour in added value.[15] This means that companies such as Internet giant Amazon perform the same tasks with far fewer staff than, for example, the Walmart supermarket group does – something that one senses intuitively. However, researchers have

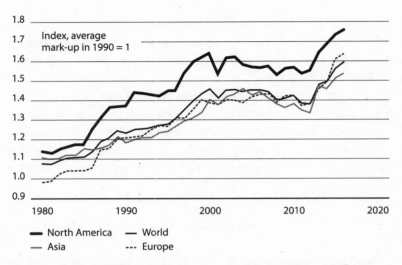

Figure 2.7   Megacompanies achieve ever-increasing margins: Mark-ups globally and in major regions

This suggests that the big players are becoming more powerful.

Source: De Loecker, Eeckhout, and Unger, "The Rise of Market Power"; https://www.brookings. edu/wp-content/uploads/2018/06/ES_THP_20180611_CompetitionFacts_20180611.pdf.

found that this particular effect of gigantism generates similar effects in a wide range of sectors. In other words, gigantism leads to a reduction in the labour component in favour of profits.

Profitability is not something that should be contested. If profits are the result of privileged positions, however, then in the long run they will be detrimental to the economy. Nor is a reduction in employment in an activity or sector necessarily detrimental to the whole economy. There may be jobs created in other activities. What is noticeable, though, is that the gigacompanies do not offer the best working conditions. After all, a dominant position can be expressed in many forms, including a *power position in the employment relationship*. Recently Amazon increased its minimum wage in the United States, undoubtedly because the Internet company is becoming aware that its salary structures are coming under fire.[16]

Wages and working conditions are a few of the aspects that are discussed in the next chapter. Gigantism has social consequences, and we must be fully aware of them. If we accept the ground rules of this

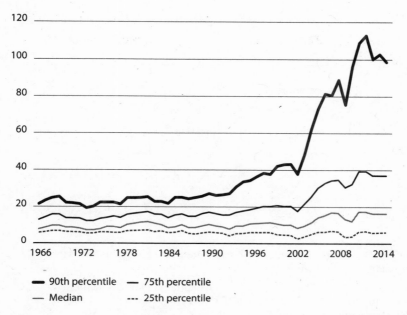

Figure 2.8   Megacorporations achieve ever-greater profits: Return on invested capital of American corporations by size, 2015

The biggest companies are also the most profitable.

Sources: Furman and Orszag, "A Firm-Level Perspective"; Koller, McKinsey, Goedhart, and Wessels, *Valuation*.

dominance, we must also recognize and accept its social consequences. The connection between social trends and the rise of gigantism may not always be drawn. Therefore, I will try to analyze some of the trends.

Research into the profitability of US companies brought the problem of abnormal profits into even sharper focus. The profits of the very largest companies (the so-called ninetieth percentile or the 10 per cent largest companies) were notably higher than those of all other companies (see figure 2.8). This trend has escalated, especially since the turn of the millennium. The abnormal upsurge in profits is a clear indication that currently, in the US economy, concentration and the balance of power are in a state of complete disarray. Inequality between businesses is worrying, with the profitability of small businesses stagnating at a low level while that of the largest groups is soaring to stratospheric heights. As if there was not enough evidence of gigantism, there are also more

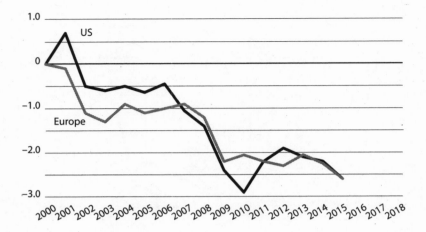

Figure 2.9 Large companies push small ones out of the economy: Monopoly formation and profitability

In both the United States and Europe the number of new companies (new enterprises as a proportion of all enterprises, cumulative change in percentage points) is falling.

Source: OECD, "Declining Business Dynamics."

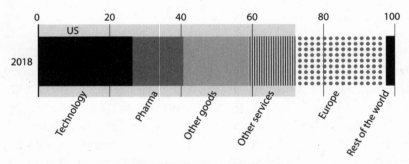

Abnormal profits = net taxed profits above 8% cost of capital, excluding goodwill, calculated for the top 5,000 listed companies.

Figure 2.10 Gigantism leads to "abnormal" profits: Breakdown of abnormal profits worldwide

Abnormal profits are mainly an American phenomenon and are largely achieved by technology and pharmaceutical companies.

Source: Bloomberg; *The Economist*, "Dynamism Has Declined across Western Economies."

and more indications that the large firms are simply pushing the smaller ones out of the economy. The number of new enterprises is declining, both in the United States and Europe (see figure 2.9). This indicates a diminishing dynamic, while the number of companies holding a monopolistic or oligopolistic position is constantly on the rise.[17]

Abnormally high profits again confirm the picture of gigantism in the economy, particularly in a number of sectors, such as technology and pharmaceuticals, especially in the United States and to a lesser extent in Europe (see figure 2.10).

Conclusion: Bigger, More Concentrated, and More Powerful

In human history there have always been examples of gigantism, but today gigantism is ubiquitous: we are not aware of it immediately and are even beginning to find it completely normal. Only when one steps back and spots the symptoms, or when they are pointed out, does one notice how the phenomenon dominates our economy and society. The economic consequences are far reaching and affect profit margins, share prices, the balance of power between regions, and the relationship between wages and capital income. Large companies make higher profits and pay more generous salaries. The largest corporations not only reduce business dynamism but also lead to less innovation and inhibit the growth of small businesses.

The United States and China are encouraging entrepreneurial gigantism, while the EU is fighting it. As a result, the EU has relatively small multinationals and is dominated by companies from other regions. The EU, however, has a culture of big government, such that social security, for example, has assumed gigantic proportions compared with that of non-EU countries. In Europe the government has replaced traditional self-reliance and has become dominant in all areas. I am not arguing for less solidarity, but I am arguing for that solidarity to be organized less by the government and more by local communities, family, and friends. Governments now institutionalize services that used to be more efficient, cheaper, and more humane. In Europe, public institutions occupy the largest and most powerful buildings: the European Central Bank in Frankfurt, the buildings of the European Union in Brussels and

Strasbourg, and the public institutions in the various member states. In the United States, power lies with the largest corporations; in Europe, with the largest bureaucracies.

While people satisfy their insatiable craving for more with larger and larger quantities of resources, engineers build bigger and bigger machines to rob the earth of its resources. Meanwhile, potentates the world over vie with each other to build the largest tower, like phallic symbols affirming their personal craving for gigantism. The economic advantages of scale and size are crucial and have served us well in the past. Economies of scale still help us, but the balance has been tipped and their disadvantages are not sufficiently taken into consideration. Economies of scale are sometimes exaggerated or end at a certain size. I am not opposed to economies of scale, but I am opposed to the excessive importance that many attach to them, and especially to the insufficient consideration of the social and environmental drawbacks, which can completely undermine the economic benefits.

3

GROWTH HORMONES
THAT PROMOTE GIGANTISM

Big, bigger, biggest. As illustrated, our economic system generates disproportionate, potent incentives for unbridled growth of organizations. Being big has become intrinsic to achieving maximum benefits and carrying minimum liabilities. Although in part this evolution may be unintentional, to an equal extent it is deliberately and subtly steered by representatives of large companies and by their lobbyists, who heavily influence policy. This need not imply a malicious hidden agenda; there is no conspiracy involving the Illuminati, the Freemasons, or the Rothschilds. Conspiracy theories are unnecessary: the impulses that encouraged gigantism are ample and originate from many directions.

In the late eighteenth century Adam Smith, one of the founders of economic theory, expressed concerns about large companies and the lack of competition. The author of *The Theory of Moral Sentiments* (1759) and *The Wealth of Nations* (1776) was preoccupied by the power of corporations. He believed that powerful companies endangered the smooth functioning of the economy. Two hundred and fifty years later, we have gone into overdrive; organizations have assumed inhuman proportions, the effects of which not only are economically and socially damaging but also have an impact on other areas such as the climate.

To fully understand why the pursuit of "big, bigger, biggest" is misguided, we must return to the roots of capitalism. Capitalism seems to have forgotten to fight its own worst enemies: a lack of competition, and too few companies with too much power. Yet it is not simply about the capitalist system; it is also about people and what makes them happy. An economy should not favour a small group at the expense of a large number of people. This analysis will give prominence to the social aspect of oversized systems. An economy on a human scale, one that makes people happier and disallows excesses, is what we seek.

This chapter explores the factors that have fuelled gigantism, from which I will draw several conclusions. The analysis is vital to understanding why this process is not easy to halt, let alone to reverse. It has become so all-pervasive, embedded in numerous systems, sometimes even translated into and thus enshrined in regulations and laws, that only a profound understanding of a myriad actors can empower us – gradually at first, then hopefully more swiftly – to bring gigantism to an end.

Four Decades of Falling Interest Rates: The World's Largest Lever

A graph says more than a thousand words (see figure 3.1). Since 1980, interest rates have declined almost continuously throughout the world. In 1980 the international interest rate was still around 13 per cent; in 2018, less than 2 per cent, and below 1 per cent in Europe and Japan. In recent years the zero limit has even turned out not to be the bottom, something which – from a purely conceptual perspective – is completely at odds with a healthy capitalist system.

Negative interest rates in a period of high inflation, as has been the case since 2021, are even more of an oddity. Such a situation can only occur if central banks manipulate interest rates. If the markets had their way, interest rates would be many percentages higher, as has been unfolding since the start of 2022, and financial turmoil is building as a consequence.

The declining interest rates have been largely the result of other important trends taking place in recent decades. First and foremost was the drop in inflation after a rapid rise in the 1970s (due in part to the oil crisis). The strong growth in productivity, the wave of globalization, and the boom in technological breakthroughs also supported falling interest rates. However, the impact of the central banks on financial markets has progressively increased, particularly since the financial crisis of 2008. Those central banks pursued a policy of steering, and intervention in, the financial markets and the economy. Interest-rate policy was a powerful weapon in this respect. Central bankers such as Alan Greenspan and Ben Bernanke in the United States and Mario Draghi in Europe systematically lowered interest rates in an attempt to postpone problems such as debt burdens and bring forward consumption and investments to support the economy.

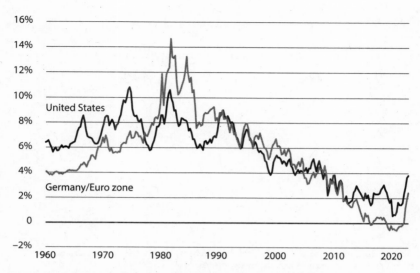

Figure 3.1   Falling interest rates creates massive leverage effect: Evolution of interest rates internationally

Source: Refinitiv Financial Datastream.

After all, declining rates mean taking an advance on the future and shifting liabilities to a distant horizon. How does that work? If interest rates fall, borrowing is easier. Companies, families, and governments can then use the extra debt to buy goods and services they would otherwise have been unable to afford until later without first having saved or increased their earnings. Obviously, companies and governments can also increase their investments when interest rates are lower, and that is positive – unless it causes overcapacity, which exacerbates the problems. Cheap money can also lead to non-productive investments: large infrastructure works that go unused (so-called white elephants), ghost towns, or other wastage of resources such as asset bubbles. Falling interest rates also have a huge leverage effect: that leverage allows you to grow faster than would be possible without loans. Falling interest rates therefore push up valuations on the stock markets; companies that therefore have a high share price can easily buy other (smaller or unlisted) companies. The chain reaction triggered by declining interest rates should therefore not be underestimated, but that is precisely what the central banks did.

An enforced drop in the interest rates engineered by central banks may appear to be a miracle cure, but it is not. It only shifts the timing of

Table 3.1   Low interest rates act like steroids: Interest and debt

Debt (USD)	Interest level (%)	Interest payment (USD)
100	7.0	7
116	6.0	7
200	3.5	7
233	3.0	7
300	2.5	7
350	2.0	7
400	1.8	7
500	1.4	7
600	1.2	7
700	1.0	7

A fall in the interest rate from 2% to 1% doubles debt capacity. A rise of interest rates
from 1% to 3% reduces debt capacity by two-thirds. Giants rise when interest rates drop,
and shrink when interest rates rise.

revenues and costs or the timing of investments. The benefits (growth, consumption, and so forth) come sooner, the disadvantages (paying off debts, decreasing overconsumption, and overcapacity) come later.

Low interest rates therefore have major consequences: they act like steroids for the economy (see table 3.1). Like performance-enhancing drugs (PEDs), they are addictive and have adverse health effects. To complete the comparison with PEDs, performance enhancers have positive effects in the short term but also numerous harmful effects in the long term. In addition, they literally skew the competition: they give an unfair edge to participants whose natural strengths and balances are insufficient to allow them to compete. In sports, steroids give athletes an advantage over those who are "natural." The same applies in economics: companies that borrow, or get a very high stock price from the stock market, have an unfair advantage. They can buy the smaller companies, drive them out, or undercut them. That kind of capitalism was not what the founding fathers had in mind; rather, it is predatory capitalism, the right of the strongest.

A fall in the interest rate from 7 per cent to 1 per cent makes seven times more debt possible. This means that companies, governments, and consumers can borrow seven times more and still only have to bear the same interest burden. The problem is not the burden of interest but the repayment of principal at the end. That is the danger of debt accumulation. As the simple example in table 3.1 shows, the effect here is not linear but exponential. A drop in interest rates from 7 per cent to 6 per cent only causes debt capacity to increase by 16 per cent. But a drop in interest rates from 2 per cent to 1 per cent increases capacity by 100 per cent, or double. Converted into dollars, a fall in interest rates from 7 per cent to 6 per cent increases debt capacity by USD 16. But a drop in interest rates from 2 per cent to 1 per cent causes debt capacity to increase by USD 350 – that is, from USD 350 to USD 700. One can imagine the leverage that this creates among countries that can borrow (such as the United States and most of the euro area countries) and corporations (especially the largest corporations, which can borrow easily). Financed by debt, they are able to make innumerable acquisitions.

Companies that can borrow more cheaply can make larger acquisitions while paying less interest. Interest rates for large corporations are systematically lower than for smaller companies. Banks and financial markets regard small and medium-sized enterprises (SMEs) as riskier and penalize them because their debt securities involve smaller amounts that are less easy to trade and involve higher fixed costs. Hence, the leverage effect is even greater for larger companies.

Since the financial crisis that erupted in 2007–08, many central banks have also launched so-called buy-back programs: they buy debt from governments and corporations. As such debt securities only exist for large companies, central banks may finance new debt issuances through their buy-back programs, thus allowing large conglomerates to finance their acquisitions. It is an example of how policy makes "big, bigger, biggest" and hence encourages gigantism.

The number of mergers and acquisitions (M&A) has increased dramatically in recent decades. Companies such as AB InBev, Facebook, Google/Alphabet, and Microsoft have become giants because, among other things, they have swallowed up other large corporations. Large companies are always looking for acquisitions, great and small, and even have entire departments devoted to M&A. In a relatively short time, the Belgian brewer AB InBev, for example, transformed into a mammoth brewery that includes Anheuser-Busch, Interbrew, Corona, and SABMiller. This expansion was largely financed by new debt secured at very low interest rates. We see the same thing in almost every sector. If we dive into the history of the past one hundred and fifty years, we

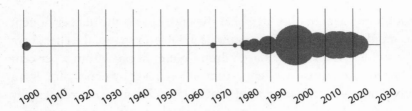

Figure 3.2   Mergers and acquisitions, 1900–2021

Fatal attraction: mergers and acquisitions are largely a feature of the last few decades. Global mergers and acquisitions in excess of USD 10 billion, inflation adjusted at 2017. The size of the bubbles corresponds with the size of the transactions.

Source: Data based on Wikipedia list of the largest mergers and acquisitions.

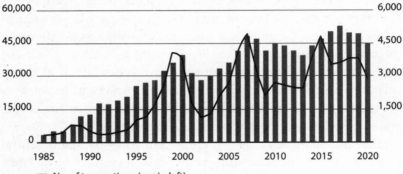

■ No. of transactions (y axis, left)
— Value of transactions in USD billions (y axis, right)

Figure 3.3   A tsunami of mergers and acquisitions: Number and value of mergers and acquisitions worldwide

The number and value of mergers and acquisitions transactions worldwide have increased dramatically over the past twenty years. Since 2000, there have been over 790,000 deals, worth USD 60,000 billion.

Source: Data based on Institute for Mergers, Acquisitions and Alliances, 2022, https://imaa-institute.org/mergers-and-acquisitions-statistics/

are struck by the amount of massive mergers that have taken place over the last four decades, a trend that had been absent for some time (see figures 3.2 and 3.3).

The list of the largest acquisitions from the past hundred years highlights this point: not only did the largest acquisitions (converted to today's dollars, and with the exception of AOL's acquisition of Time Warner at the peak of the Internet bubble) occur most recently, but also the sheer number of large transactions has grown exponentially. That is exactly what one would expect from the interest-rate stimulus and the debt leverage, which give large companies in particular a significant advantage. We have become so accustomed to these megatransactions that they are no longer questioned. Are they healthy? Are they normal in a capitalist system? Should brakes be imposed?

Too many players make huge sums of money from these transactions. Increasingly, governments also see national interests in these mergers and will block them if they believe (rightly or wrongly) that national interests are at stake. But no one defends the interests of the employee, customer, supplier, or new competitor. Europe or especially the United States rarely argues that free competition is threatened. Small (symbolic) segments of the acquisition must be sold off, now and then, as a peace offering, but the big deal remains intact. As a consequence, the free market has changed entirely and at breakneck speed during the past decades.

Many of these big mergers and acquisitions are motivated by economies of scale or synergy effects. In other words, the top managers are convinced that one and one does not make two but that merging two separate companies will form a whole that is larger than the sum of its parts. These synergies may have not only cost advantages (economies of scale) but also increased revenues because the merged company will be able to offer more products in more markets, for example, or because the diversification effects or variety of knowledge can be shared in the new and larger entity.

A study by the consultancy firm Bain & Company,[1] however, shows that 70 per cent of the companies that make an acquisition overestimate the synergies. As a result, the actual value created by M&A has frequently been questioned more by academics than by business consultants. According to the management journal *Harvard Business Review*, 60 per cent of all M&A fail.[2] Academic studies even report failure rates of up to 83 per cent.[3]

Although synergies are often the main reason for M&A, CEOs like to see themselves as empire builders. They are keen to build up a larger company and are often encouraged to do so by bonus or option systems. In recent decades many companies were built by ego-driven CEOs, only to subsequently implode. Dexia, Tyco, Fortis, AOL Time Warner, Deutsche Bank, and DaimlerChrysler spring to mind. In the hands of a hubristic CEO, today's cheap money is a weapon of self-destruction for healthy businesses.

Another consequence of interest rates (which are still too low but have been rising since 2022) and the opportunity to finance takeovers with free money is that a string of companies can operate at a loss for an incredibly long time. This has enabled new business models in which a company can secure sufficient funding to upend completely another company or an entire sector, survive the disruption, and then exploit a monopoly or near-monopoly situation. I am thinking of Uber, Amazon, Zalando, and Netflix. Such an economic strategy was impossible when the cost of capital was much higher and the economy was not flooded with masses of liquidity. However, this new form of dumping falls between the cracks of the current economic rules. The media, retail, and tourism sectors are just the tip of the iceberg. Most sectors can become entangled in a price war by a giant that first destroys margins, drives companies out of business, and then relegates them to the economic desert.

Recently there has been a growing awareness that acquisitions by giants are unhealthy for economic dynamics. Megacorporations that devour small companies execute what are called predatory acquisitions or killer acquisitions – just as Champions League clubs buy young players from smaller clubs to put on the bench; by doing so, they prevent their smaller counterparts from becoming rivals because those clubs simply cannot afford to keep young, world-class talent. Gigacorporations pursue the same tactics, gobbling up young, promising companies before they can become a real threat. Cheap money and the power of a high stock-market value make it an unfair fight.

Globalization

The expansion of globalization in recent decades has galvanized the advance of gigantism. The world economy has evolved from a game dominated by the "triad" regions – Western Europe, the United States, and Japan – into a global economy whose dimensions have been completely changed by China, other Asian countries, and (after the fall of the Berlin Wall) the whole of Eastern Europe. A bigger playing field leads to bigger players. We saw this when the unification of the euro area gave rise to very large banks, but it occurs in all regions and all eras. Globalization is a powerful engine of gigantism.

The European Union, the euro, and the euro area, for example, were created specifically to have an internal market equal to that of the United States and thus to form larger companies. So, instead of national and smaller champions, big European equivalents that could compete with the American multinationals were created. This was not faulty reasoning, but "size" was a specific goal and thus a significant driver of a sought-after European gigantism. If there had been no euro area, and if the European Central Bank had not turned a blind eye (had not devised incentive policies) to the creation of global financial players, Europe would never have had the gigantic banks that caused the now-familiar troubles in 2008 (the "too big to fail" phenomenon). Deutsche Bank, BNP Paribas, ING, SocGen, and many others were then in the running to challenge the hegemony of Goldman Sachs, JP Morgan, or Morgan Stanley.

Globalization arose as a consequence of the benefits of free trade. No economist is against free trade as such. The fact that countries trade and specialize in the things in which they have a competitive advantage offers benefits to all trading partners, but the impact this has in many areas has been either entirely underestimated or not supported adequately. Free trade without the equivalent rules and protection in social security creates distortions. Economists' simplified models do not include social security, product safety standards, or carbon dioxide emissions. All these major side effects are, therefore, a result not of unbridled capitalism but of unbridled gigantism. Pure capitalism values competition, fairness, and responsibility over externalities.

Gigantism, and its impact on the environment and society, is simply one corollary of globalization. Later, when I talk about solutions, I will not be arguing in favour of antiglobalization. I have paid close attention to the antiglobalists; in their desperation they veto the entire system, which is tantamount to throwing the baby out with the bathwater. We can, however, embrace the global while simultaneously promoting the local. In any case, multinational companies have benefited most from globalization. Their scale, growth, profits, and impact have soared thanks to open borders and the broadening of the trading arena. A company that is able to take the step of expanding its activities globally – either on its own or through M&A – sees its impact and size swell disproportionately. This gives rise to a duality in the business world: local players and global champions. The former increasingly fall prey to the latter. At the same time, a sort of beauty contest is also underway, seeking to lure global champions with all kinds of benefits, for which local companies will ultimately have to pay. The time is ripe to rethink globalization.

Companies, Especially the Giants,
Pay Less and Less Tax

Large companies pay less and less tax. The graph showing the drop in interest rates since 1980 (see figure 3.1) is easy to remember: it shows a steady decline. The drop in worldwide corporate income tax rates almost mirrors the decrease in interest rates (see figure 3.4 and table 3.2). Since the end of the Second World War the average rate of corporate tax in the OECD countries has almost halved, and this decline continued after the 2008 financial crisis. In some sectors, such as technology, the average corporate tax rate is even lower.

The decrease in corporate tax rates is due to several factors. For instance, the starting point was quite high. The main causes of the parallel decline in all countries and regions are globalization and the global knowledge and organization of the lobby that these corporations can set up. The multinationals started playing different countries off against each other when deciding where to make their next big investments. After all, they know better than the individual countries which tax regimes, subsidies, and other advantages such as permits or sites they can acquire here and there. Such location decisions can bring a great number of jobs to a country (think of automobile assembly), so countries have become ensnared in a sort of international competition. Countries want to score well in the comparative tables used, and taxes play a major role in the process, as do qualitative factors. To establish the headquarters of a multinational, world leaders bend over backwards, and CEOs are received as heads of state. They are also offered benefits in the form of direct subsidies, free land, or assistance with permits. In the recent past, many countries received Elon Musk like royalty to entice him to locate his e-battery plant or e-car manufacturing line there. In the United States, Musk pitted the states against one another when he moved his headquarters from California to Texas.

Significantly, the United States was not the leader in low corporate taxes until a few years ago, something that changed dramatically under President Donald Trump. Historically, the United States had one of the highest corporate tax rates. The country played a minor role in the "beauty contests" as a recipient of investment. Rather, American companies had an international expansion model and actively participated in those competitions, playing the countries off against each other to gain optimal conditions for establishment. Other countries

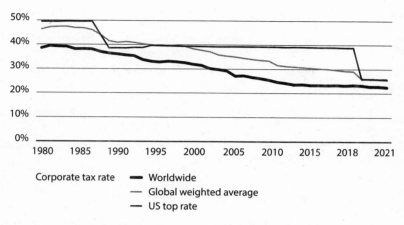

Figure 3.4   Large companies pay less and less tax: Corporate tax rate, worldwide and in the United States

Source: Tax Foundation, based on data from PWC, KPMG, and Deloitte, https://taxfoundation. org/publications/corporate-tax-rates-around-the-world/.

Table 3.2   Corporate taxes are low and have continued to fall since the crisis: Corporate taxes, as a percentage of profits

OECD		US			
1980	2019	1950	1985	1995	2019
50%	<25%	50%	40%	30%	20%

and regions played a pioneering role in the reduction of corporate tax rates. The development of the European Union, for instance, was a factor, with each member state competing with other EU members and offering favorable tax regimes in a bid to poach corporations from each other.

Little by little, this international beauty contest has created a large divide between taxes for large companies and those for smaller (mostly local) companies. The latter do not participate in contests of that kind, anyway, and thus need not be appeased with tax breaks. Similarly, in recent decades countries have always preferred a drop in corporate income tax to a drop in personal income tax (see figure 3.5). This effect accelerated after the financial crisis.

After 2008, governments had to contend with rising government deficits and a shrinking economy. They then chose to pursue a pro-entrepreneurship policy and, by doing so, stole businesses or activities

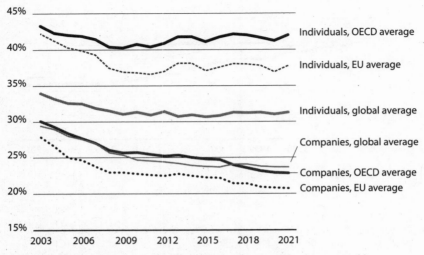

Figure 3.5   Companies pay less tax than citizens do: Actual taxes paid by companies and individuals

Source: Data based on KPMG Tax Rates Online tool, https://home.kpmg/xx/en/home/services/tax/tax-tools-and-resources/tax-rates-online.html; Toplensky, "Multinationals Pay Lower Taxes."

from other countries. For individual taxpayers, the tax burden increased. As said, large companies pay substantially less tax than small, local companies do, yet relatively little is done to close this inequitable gap. The explanation is simple: multinationals cultivate far closer ties with policy-makers. In 2021 the OECD decided to impose a minimum tax of 15 per cent on multinational companies.[4] This was certainly a step forward and calls a halt to the "race to the bottom." Meanwhile, calls to raise the corporate tax rate for gigacorporations (particularly the tech giants) are more insistent – principally in the EU, but also in the United States.

Europe had (before Brexit) some 31,000 Eurocrats, and there are also 30,000 lobbyists in the European capital, Brussels. There are 12,000 official lobbyists in Washington, although researchers estimate the number at 90,000, excluding support staff.[5] This means that, in Europe as well as in the United States, there is a multitude of lobbyists for every politician, and every civil servant can, in principle, be targeted by a lobbyist. The small business lobby is of much less importance, whether in Washington or in Brussels. Small businesses have neither the resources nor the political clout to make their case and play a role in policy. Their

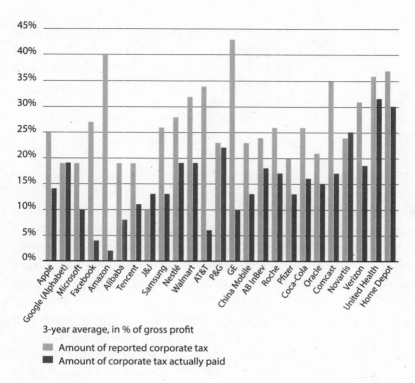

3-year average, in % of gross profit

▨ Amount of reported corporate tax
■ Amount of corporate tax actually paid

Figure 3.6   Large companies pay less tax than they claim: Corporate tax rates of the world's largest corporations

Source: UBS and *Financial Times* calculations based on 2017 figures

CEOs are neither found at the World Economic Forum in Davos or other international summits nor offered a post in the highest governing bodies of a central bank or an international institution. Optimizing taxes across countries is a specialist job for which multinationals call on teams of their own experts and tax consultants. The world's largest companies do not pay ordinary corporate tax rates. Moreover, they succeed in reporting higher tax rates than they actually pay (see figure 3.6). In some countries, such as Ireland, they maintain reserves that have yet to be taxed or that can ultimately be used for other purposes (such as take-overs, and buy-backs of their own shares).

Lower corporate taxes have a massive effect on gigantism. They result in lower capital costs for large companies; far more resources remain within the company, for example, for investment, for acquisitions, or for better remuneration of staff. By now, the reader will realize that large companies receive injections of growth hormones from all kinds of sources and that this can set a growth sprint in motion Multinationals continue to expand and enjoy numerous competitive advantages that small businesses can only dream of.

The Regulator, Friend of Big Business

Whether intentionally or not, the government plays a role either in encouraging companies to expand or in favouring large corporations. Regulations, for instance, are frequently tailored to multinationals; unlike small businesses, they can handle such complex rules. Complexity is a powerful impetus for "bigness," and governments with their regulations create enormous complexity. In a *De Tijd* newspaper interview in 2017, the chief of one of the four largest audit and consulting companies said, "Regulations? We love them!" They are the powerhouse of large consulting firms. For this reason, the lobbies of a number of sectors with large companies is pushing for ever-increasing regulation, preferring new rules and complex supervision to simple and strictly controlled rules. The government is an inexhaustible source of new regulations and also wants companies to comply with them. This has obliged them to create functions to ensure compliance with government regulations. Compliance functions are an enormous burden for small companies, while multinationals can easily fit them into their existing structures. That is why large groups have fewer problems with new regulations; they realize that they form an entry barrier to competition and thus protect their position. Governments should be aware of this, particularly when they make timid attempts to encourage local companies.

Subsidies are another form of growth hormone for large companies. They can afford to hire subsidy experts who not only know about subsidies (SMEs often do not hear about subsidy opportunities) but can also systematically initiate the grant application procedures. Large companies also have powerful lobbying machines and excellent contacts with governments and can advocate for subsidy systems that suit them best. The major recovery plans, climate plans, and neo-Marshall plans are all cut to fit the requirements of the largest corporations. This is another reason that COVID-19 was a powerful catalyst for gigantism, complemented by all the recent climate plans such as the European Green Deal. Most of these funds are focused on the largest corporations.

Technology Platforms

The largest companies in the world today are the tech giants. Apple, Amazon, Google, Microsoft, and Facebook are probably the best-known examples, but there are also Chinese counterparts such as Alibaba, Tencent, and Ctrip. Specifically, one could say that the largest corporations are *platform* businesses: they offer a platform where users can find or use a plethora of services and products. These companies optimize the advantages of gigantism: their growth is turbo-charged by the afore-mentioned benefits coupled with the speed of technology, which allows them to bundle customers and make other companies dependent on them.

The tech companies are careful not to encroach too much on each other's domains; they each have their own space where they can build a quasi-monopoly. There are minor overlaps, but these are generally of a cosmetic nature. In fact, they have great respect for each other's specialization and dominance. They also avoid sectors that traditionally have a highly organized lobby (pharma, finance, car manufacturing) not for fear of competition but for fear of their lobbying the government against them. If the traditional sectors felt threatened, there would be a more urgent demand to curb the power of the tech giants.

In addition to the well-known giants, there are a number of growing niche players. In those niches, companies are very often aggregators of fragmented activities. Booking.com takes a 10 to 25 per cent margin on each hotel booking – even up to 60 per cent if a hotel wants to appear high on the list. Since the search engines lead tourists to Booking.com, online searches for a holiday destination run almost automatically through these platform businesses. They thus take a commission on global tourism, a sector that is highly fragmented and very poorly organized. Technology makes it fairly easy to control global activities that were once far more fragmented. The platform business model is also emerging in the hospitality and distribution sectors. Platform companies take large commissions on local activities that are poorly organized.

As these platform companies are organized internationally, it is not always clear whether or not they pay the same local taxes. Airbnb, Uber, Amazon, and LinkedIn, to name but a few, have become gateways to local economic activities but take commissions that are whisked off abroad. They have become giants in markets where, until recently, this kind of gigantism was generally absent.

Crony Capitalism

Governments also deploy means other than regulations to foster corporate growth. They promote the idea that "big is beautiful." Large corporations in the United States finance the election of presidential candidates. Governments also prefer to work with large companies on their own projects. The state's information technology assets are managed or developed not by the local SME but by the likes of Siemens, IBM, Oracle, or SAP. Small businesses simply cannot meet the official requirements, which are custom-made for multinationals. In addition, the government does not always pay its bills promptly, something an SME cannot always survive. Big government prefers big corporations.

Crony capitalism also creates problems for the economy. It means that capitalism is no longer pure but unstable. The distance between the companies and the government has narrowed considerably, and one's connections with the government determine whether or not one is successful. Indeed, the entanglement of big business and politics is evident in several ways. For example, after their time in power, politicians often work for large financial concerns such as Goldman Sachs, Uber, big private equity firms, utility companies, or other enterprises that require good relations with the government. This revolving door works both ways because many key roles in government-related institutions are held by individuals from the same companies.

Exclusive summits such as the World Economic Forum in Davos or the Bilderberg conferences have their shortcomings. Although invaluable for gaining new ideas or making contacts, they also serve as an ideal biotope for crony capitalism. SMEs have neither the means (an entrance ticket can cost hundreds of thousands of euros, and the higher the price, the higher you can network), nor the invitation (Bilderberg and other conferences are by invitation only).

This makes the links between politics and business extremely one-sided. Our decision makers only hear the big corporations and thus equate their interests with those of the economy. This approach seeps through not only in all kinds of regulations and guidelines but also in referrals to large companies and in the formation of networks. Unless they are undergoing unprecedented growth and might join the ranks of big companies in the future, SMEs rarely take tea with a minister or president.

Big Feels Safe

Most of the "big-makers" I have cited are related to macroeconomic factors and government behaviour. But human beings also tend to opt for safety, and most consider large companies to be safer than small ones – safer in the sense that there is less risk of something going wrong or of non-standard quality, or, if something does go wrong, the company guarantees to remedy the defects. We are inclined to see large corporations as less likely to fail. To some extent this is true: they are more diversified, often have a long history, and have structures that have weathered a few storms. In this sense, one can certainly argue in favour of choosing big. We also tend to feel safer on large planes and large ships, although clearly the *Titanic* disproved that. And, although large companies may seem more remote, that hardly plays a role in the choice of bulk goods or mainstream services.

So, to win customers, small businesses need to focus on other aspects: quality, a niche, a specialty, or price. Even after the financial crisis, relatively few small banks were able to lure customers away from large financial institutions. The customers realized that governments were more prepared to rescue the large banks than the smaller ones. The same situation occurs when large companies – steel companies in the past or, more recently, the automotive industry – run into problems. Governments go to great lengths to keep those entities afloat, providing them with all kinds of benefits, government grants, and tax breaks. When a large company closes its doors, the news is in all the media. When thousands of jobs disappear at small businesses, no one bats an eye.

As mentioned earlier, small businesses pay higher interest rates and more taxes. Banks regard them as a higher risk, not always because of their size but sometimes because of the sector in which they operate. For example, there are more small enterprises in the construction, hotel, and catering industries, which are characterized by high volatility and cyclical sensitivity. Apart from these objective reasons, SMEs are considered riskier because they are younger, supported by a few key figures rather than a broad organization, and less diversified or because their reporting is not yet as good as that of large companies. A small company has a great deal to prove, which means that it does not always receive support at critical moments, which in turn makes bankruptcy inevitable. Small companies are thus trapped in a self-fulfilling spiral:

the risks they run are de facto higher because the world at large does not accept the same risks from a small company as it does from a large corporation. In turn, this makes smaller companies less attractive to talented staff; working for a large corporation is perceived as less risky. Combined with better terms of employment, this leads to a distorted competitive situation.

Insufficient Action against Global Cartels

Laws to stimulate competition are not a modern invention; such legislation was first introduced in Roman times. The Romans knew that competition was important to ensure that the prices of consumables, such as agricultural products and food, were affordable. Monopolies and price fixing are at the root of excessive prices or artificial scarcity. In the year 301, Emperor Diocletian (244–311 CE) passed a law imposing the death penalty on anyone who attempted to manipulate prices. Antitrust laws have been a constant throughout Western history. In the United States the Sherman Antitrust Act of 1890 aimed to put a stop to large conglomerates that made price-fixing deals. Monopolies were also prohibited. That legislation was far reaching: "Every person who shall monopolize, or attempt to monopolize [...] any area of the trade or commerce [...] shall be deemed guilty of a misdemeanor."[6] That is quite a deterrent. However, enforcing the law proved problematic, and in the following years J.P. Morgan and Andrew Carnegie became the richest people in the world by creating monopolies.

In his book *The Curse of Bigness*, Tim Wu thoroughly analyzes this aspect of gigantism and comes to the conclusion, as I do, that the economy must be organized on a human scale. He advances the tenets of Louis Brandeis, the US Supreme Court justice in the early twentieth century. Brandeis was concerned about the emergence of large industrial companies that developed a quasi-monopoly position, in defiance of the Sherman Act. He also recognized that this threatened innovation and social rights. He was proved right on a number of issues and as a result gained more support from politicians. It played a role in the American elections of 1912, in which Theodore Roosevelt took on Woodrow Wilson. The battle was between those in favour of large corporations' dominance and its opponents, who wanted to tackle it by cracking down on large corporations' privileges and corruption. Roosevelt, however, won. Brandeis's thesis can be traced back directly to Adam Smith's concerns about fairness and ethics. Brandeis was worried about the plight of ordinary people and the economic conditions in which they lived and the impact of the economy on one's character and, ultimately, on the soul of the nation. When the economy is organized for the benefit of big corporations, it creates frustration that eventually translates into populism and extremism. All of this sounds all too familiar when you consider the rise of Trumpism in the last decade. Trumpism thrives in a climate of gigantism in which the individual feels neglected and the gap between rich and poor is growing. Wu ends his analysis, which starts from a very different perspective, with the conclusion that it is better to keep things manageable and limited. *The Curse of Bigness* thus also values the advantages of the modest, the local, and the smaller over the economy of the titans.

In Europe, since the creation of the European Union, there has been a policy of combating cartels and monopolies. Article 85 of the EC Treaty prohibits price fixing, and Article 86 deals with monopolies. The difficulty lies in enforcing that legislation. Both in the United States and in Europe antitrust laws have been rendered toothless. Whereas in the past, large companies in important sectors were broken up because of their dominant position, this has not been successful in recent decades, despite attempts to do so.

At the beginning of the twentieth century John D. Rockefeller's Standard Oil Company was one of the most powerful companies in the United States, and Rockefeller himself was the nation's richest man. Yet his enterprise was broken up in 1911 after the courts ruled that Standard Oil had a monopoly. The company was split into thirty-four smaller companies, of which ExxonMobil and Chevron are still well-known brand names today. Another example is the splitting up of the powerful Bell Telephone Company. In 1982 this giant, then called AT&T, was divided into seven smaller "Baby Bells" or regional telephone companies. As well as AT&T Corp., Verizon Communications has also remained a household name.

In 1999, Microsoft was caught in the crosshairs of the Sherman Act, and legal proceedings were instituted against the software giant. It was accused of monopolizing the personal-computer market and the operating system sector and merging an operating system with a search engine (Internet Explorer). In a first ruling, the court stated that Microsoft had indeed been guilty of monopoly formation. The court obliged the company to split into two parts: one branch dedicated to operating systems, and the other to writing software programs. However, Microsoft appealed, and in 2001 the judgment was diluted after Microsoft promised that other software systems besides Word, Excel, and PowerPoint would also be able to run on the Windows platforms. Although this is all theoretically possible, it is now abundantly clear that the monopoly remains in place, and any innovations by new players have been unable to penetrate that market.

The Microsoft case was a watershed in antitrust law. If Microsoft had been split up, the situation for the other tech giants would have been completely different today. Perhaps Microsoft had a lucky day. At the time of the ruling, the technology sector was booming; there was even talk of a technology bubble. But by the time Microsoft appealed the court ruling, the technology bubble was bursting and the US economy was in recession – a malaise that was compounded by the 11 September 2001 attacks on the Twin Towers of the World Trade Center in New York and on the Pentagon building in Washington. Perhaps no one wanted even more chaos, or perhaps the Americans wished to consolidate their leading technological position.

Others place the tipping point much earlier, in the 1980s. The legal specialist and academic Robert Bork became known in 1987 when, after a days-long smear campaign, a majority of US senators prevented him from getting a seat on the US Supreme Court. Yet he was an eminent jurist and was nominated by the president himself. But President Ronald Reagan had been weakened by the Iran-Contra scandal and no longer had the courage to challenge it. Bork had had a big impact on antitrust rulings in previous years: he was an opponent of strict cartel rulings, believing that they over-protected small business owners and were therefore more expensive for consumers. Simply put: large companies are more efficient, and the consumer benefits from this in the form of lower prices, which increases consumer welfare. This became the new norm in the assessment of possible cartels: if consumers stood to gain, a merger should not be blocked. It marked the onset of a vast wave of acquisitions and a marked reduction in the legal blocking of such mergers by the US Department of Justice and the Federal Trade Commission.

Thus, whereas in the early years of capitalism, large, powerful companies were regularly broken up, this has not happened in recent decades, despite the fact that oligopolies or even monopolies have clearly been formed in several important sectors of the new technology. Such formations not only lead to overly expensive products and services, and monopoly profits for those producers, but also to less innovation from the new, large players.

In April 2018 the US Senate grilled Mark Zuckerberg, the CEO of Facebook, about various practices of the social networking company. The questions were rather tame and primarily demonstrated that the older senators were ill acquainted with new technology. Nevertheless, the Facebook top executive became a little hot under the collar, particularly when Senator Lindsey Graham asked him if he could name one competitor. Zuckerberg could not but managed to circumvent the question of whether Facebook qualified as a monopoly under the Sherman Act. Graham then asked him whether he thought Facebook was a monopoly. Zuckerberg responded nonchalantly, "It certainly doesn't feel like that to me."

As the lobby of large corporations has now become immensely powerful, the Sherman Act – and by extension all antitrust efforts – has been weakened in the United States. Globalization is also involved; the market in question is rarely the home market. Consequently, national regulators hesitate to trim the size of their national champions. To do so would impede their international strength, and, with their corporate giants compromised, foreign rivals could encroach upon their home markets with greater ease.

Until recently, antitrust interventions in Europe were fairly mild. However, they were still more draconian than in the United States (see figure 3.7).[7] The national champions were also smaller than their American counterparts because the economies of scale following the formation of the EU and the euro area were slower to develop than the similar phenomenon on the other side of the Atlantic. National antitrust laws also kept some companies small, making them easy prey for takeover by national champions from larger countries within the Union or from the United States. Recently China has also launched an impressive takeover spree in Europe, scouting for small national champions such as the Swedish automobile brand Volvo or Austrian

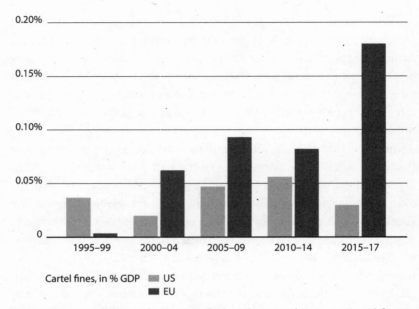

Figure 3.7   Europe is tougher on cartels than the United States is. Cartel fines:
United States versus Europe

Source: Gutiérrez and Philippon, "How EU Markets Became More Competitive."

aircraft manufacturer Diamond Aircraft Industries; also on China's wish
list are utilities and financial institutions.

It is futile to search for a global antitrust court; the world may have
globalized, but strong international institutions have not followed suit
to the same extent. Or else these institutions are populated with people
who cut their teeth working for the corporate giants, which means they
have also lost their bite.

The natural home of the sequoia, the world's largest tree, is the coast
of California in the United States. The giant sequoia owes its growth
and size to a favorable microclimate; copious amounts of sunlight,
coupled with a year-round supply of moisture from the ocean, assure
a steady dosage of growth hormones. Scientists also point to another
key factor, however, without which the sequoia would be simply an
ordinary, big tree: *the sequoia has no competition*, a feature it shares with
whales, sharks, elephants, dinosaurs, and even tarantulas. The absence
of members of their own species in their immediate vicinity facilitates
their potential for exponential growth.

Too Big to Fail

When things go wrong with a giant company, the card of "too big to fail" is often played. This concept was particularly evident during the financial crisis, when large banks seemed to be dropping like flies. They were rescued, some quite blatantly – like the Dutch ING and the Belgian-French Dexia – and others through surreptitious buy-up programs of their toxic paper in the United States and Europe, by the respective central banks. Large banks must not be allowed to fail because it "could catastrophically damage the financial system and the economy." Also in other sectors – car manufacturing, steel, aviation, and chemicals – large companies can count on extra support if the crisis becomes life threatening.

The idea that the collapse of one company could cause an entire sector, and eventually the entire economy, to crumble is not only grotesque and exaggerated (it would have been better if a few large banks had officially gone bankrupt and broken up into smaller, healthy banks), but also a vicious circle. Large financial players are thus encouraged to become big enough to be deemed too big to fail. In other sectors, one senses that companies are trying to achieve the same status. Car manufacturers are vital for the labour market, telecom companies are vital for the communication system, some iconic companies are vital for a nation's "brand," and so forth. This "too big to fail" thinking is fatal to the regeneration of an economy; the real transformation of sectors and activities will never happen if the established players are granted immortal status. Innovation is curtailed, and consumers and citizens pay too high a price, for too long, for an inferior service or product.

In the financial sector, for example, many institutions have been called too big to fail since 2008 and have simply remained too big. In 2022, Deutsche Bank was still too big and, above all, too arrogant. Little effort has been made to shrink those "too big to fail" banks as a means to pre-empt future damage but most of all to introduce more competition into the sector. Only the players from small countries – such as Belgium, the Netherlands, Ireland, and Iceland – were substantially downsized. But the big countries kept their big institutions; the taxpayers and the consumers footed the bill.

Big Data

A new growth stimulus for large companies is their possession of big data: the wealth of information about their customers, their spending behaviour, search histories, and possible interests. This gives them an enormous advantage over smaller companies and newcomers, who do not have this information or have yet to build it. Moreover, small players lack the infrastructure and resources to analyze such big data.

Some initiatives to make this information public (so-called open source) mostly fail because there is no economic incentive to simply share the information. There is one obstacle with which big data must contend, however, and that is the limits imposed by data privacy. This straitjacket is particularly tight in Europe, which has, for example, prevented large data owners – such as financial institutions – from using it on a massive scale. It is only a matter of time, though, before they will use this big data within the permitted framework to thwart the entry of entities such as social media giants into their sector.

Increasing Global Population

For a long time the world's population hovered at around one billion people. The growth explosion during the last forty years has set us on a path towards a global population of ten billion. A planet that is home to one billion inhabitants is clearly very differently organized than one with seven or eight billion denizens.

This demographic rise exerts tremendous pressure on the planet, particularly if most of the world's citizens aspire to a lifestyle such as that enjoyed in the West. To ensure the worldwide availability of all these products and services, governments are pinning their hopes on large corporations. But corporations are not the only entities being encouraged to "go big." Non-governmental organizations have also begun to organize themselves as gigantic multinationals. Aside from their normal activities, they invest heavily in lobbying, which induces them to behave precisely as the multinationals they so often detest. The bigger NGOs grow, the likelier they are to derail, as we have witnessed often in recent years.

Population growth is one of the main engines of gigantism, and of the phenomena that go hand in hand with it, such as megacities. The

Figure 3.8   The new giants of the sea: Large container ships

population growth of some continents (think of Africa) will present huge challenges. Singapore is currently building a much larger port, which is intended to facilitate trade between Africa and China in the next fifty years. Is that visionary? Perhaps a quick look at the demographic forecasts was sufficient to fuel ambitious plans to turn the Port of Singapore into a giant trans-shipment port.

A hundred years ago Africa was still a continent with fewer inhabitants than Europe. By the end of this century Africa will have a population eight times larger than that of Europe and, with four billion inhabitants, will be a close runner-up to the most populous continent, Asia. A larger population requires larger ports. Larger ports cooperate with other large ports and stimulate the demand for larger ships (see figure 3.8). Large ships are built in gigantic shipyards and require gigantic engines. Such large, complex engines can only be built thanks to an enormous amount of engineering power, which only large companies can handle. Large ports, large airports, large aircraft, and large organizations – gigantism is ubiquitous, but we do not sufficiently realize the connections and motives that propel this process to the inhuman proportions we encounter everywhere today.

Advertising Budgets

Small businesses garner little attention, even if their products or services are better than those of large companies. This is partly due to the lack of advertising and various media to attract and retain consumers' attention. A large advertising budget can, for a long time, give an inferior product a competitive advantage over a small company's superior product. My baker makes fantastic *Lierse vlaaike*, a special tart from the small Flemish city of Lier, which are probably better than many of the cookies produced by American or European multinationals such as Kellogg's, Ferrero, or Mondelez. But even if my baker wanted to prove it, he would never be able to save up the funds to bring that message to the attention of the larger world public.

I am focusing on this example, but it certainly drives home one point: advertising has been an important trigger for gigantism in several sectors. At large events like the Olympic Games, the Super Bowl (the American football finale), or the FIFA World Cup for soccer, the majors are omnipresent in an effort to maintain their market position. Often, consumers can only choose between products offered by megacorporations. By advertising en masse, these groups encourage consumers to follow their basic instinct: to choose the products they know, that they have heard of, and hence that they trust. This is another way in which size is rewarded. The consumer is bombarded by incentives to compare his local player with the big competitor – and its dazzling brand image, conceived by marketers – and dismiss the local enterprise as inferior.

Conclusion: Rampant Growth Hormones and a "Too Big to Fail" Corporate Doctrine Create Gigantism

Large companies have always existed, and, in itself, there is nothing wrong with that. But this epoch is typified by companies exploding into megaconcerns that dominate activities, sectors, and the global economy and now wield considerable power in society. Governments have little grip on these giants, partly because, through globalization, they no longer have any impact on cross-border companies, but also because these companies have become a state within the state. They are so well structured that they are able to exploit governments' weaknesses and play the various states off against each other internationally. Moreover, they have the means to foster close ties with policy-makers and almost spoon-feed them with new bills and regulations. They are simply better organized than countries and their international institutions.

As explained in this chapter, there are several factors that account for the wanton growth of the past decades. Given the myriad disproportionate advantages that large corporations have over smaller ones, it has become imperative for any business either to grow into a large enterprise or to excel in a small or local niche. But even the latter has become a tricky strategy because platform companies subject the smaller players to a form of corporate colonization. Smaller players wanting to generate revenue are in many cases compelled to pay commissions. Booking. com, Airbnb, the Apple App Store, Facebook, Amazon, Google, and increasingly their Chinese counterparts Alibaba, Ctrip, or Tencent are also active in local markets and niches as facilitators or intermediaries.

Naturally, big business has made a huge contribution to our modern economy. I neither dispute that, nor need to emphasize it at length. The point is that big businesses rose to dominance by virtue of their own excellence, but also because – perhaps unintentionally – they were supercharged by the circumstances, the regulations, and the policies.

The consequences of that gigantism are felt around the world. Everyone is aware of it intuitively, but in the following chapter I will map out these implications in detail, using the metaphor of sports, specifically football (known as soccer in the United States).

The Champions League is the competition between the largest European clubs. It has produced a phenomenon that has also emerged in various sectors and activities with far-reaching economic and social consequences.

4

THE CHAMPIONS LEAGUE EFFECT

What do the football clubs of Malmö, Bruges, Glasgow, and Porto have in common? They all played the finals of the UEFA Nations League in the 1970s and 1980s. It might not be apparent today, but, back then, teams from small countries (and hence small leagues) used to perform well. Ajax and Anderlecht, but also Vienna, Gothenburg, Aberdeen, and Mechelen, were feared opponents on the way to a European final.

Although some of these clubs rebound sporadically, and Ajax is still considered a redoubtable contender and supplier of talent, they no longer rank among the top European football leagues. Small countries used to compete for the European title, and although the larger countries won more frequently, the small clubs still had a fighting chance. Tiny little Beveren beat Inter Milan, Waterschei beat Paris Saint-Germain, and Winterslag defeated mighty Arsenal. Dutch, Belgian, Scottish, Irish, Norwegian, Austrian, and Swedish clubs regularly finished at the top. This is clear from country rankings based on club results. From the creation of the Union of European Football Associations in 1954 until 1990, small countries regularly appeared in the top five rankings. Hungary, Scotland, Belgium, and the Netherlands were among them for a sustained period.

That changed when the competitions underwent a transformation, and the Champions League was founded in 1992. Since then, over the last thirty years, a few large football countries have dominated the top three, while the number of small countries has shrunk. Germany, Italy, England, and Spain always dominate the top, switching places among themselves.

This cannot be chalked up to coincidence. The rules of the Champions League make it impossible for small clubs and small countries to compete for the title. These rules mainly relate to the redistribution of vast sums of money. Non-participants or early losers are not entitled to the gigantic pot of prize money, and therefore the gap between them and the top clubs – which are systematically able to participate in the "billion-dollar ball" – continues to widen. Every year, this effect intensifies. The winners acquire more resources and are able to buy better players, perhaps even from potential direct competitors, thereby boosting their opportunities to rake in profits. With each year that passes, the winners become stronger, and the gap between them and potential rivals expands. The Champions League pays EUR 30 million in prize money to clubs that reach the top twelve, an amount received in addition to other revenues gleaned from being in the preliminary round. A team like Futbol Club Barcelona or Liverpool FC can easily come away with EUR 80 million from the Champions League, while a club that does not go beyond the preliminaries must make do with only EUR 5 million. FC Barcelona also raises EUR 250 million in media revenue and has a total budget of EUR 1 billion.

Barcelona's players each earn an average of more than EUR 10 million per year, a total of EUR 270 million. By way of comparison, Ajax, which competed with Barcelona during the decades before the Champions League was founded, must now make do with an annual budget of EUR 90 million – roughly the same as the prize money for a team that makes it to the final twelve of the Champions League. The best young Ajax players leave the team early to join Champions League clubs, rather than competing with their Amsterdam club in the battle for a permanent spot at the top in the longer term.

I calculated the Champions League effect and translated it into a diagram, figure 4.1.

Since the creation of the Champions League in 1992, the rankings of the small countries have fallen spectacularly. At the same time, the biggest countries climbed to the top and never relinquished their places. It illustrates perfectly how a number of rules of the game – rules on which the largest countries could leave their mark - favour the clubs from large countries, after which those teams effortlessly maintain their position. The small countries and their equally modest football teams do not stand the slightest chance of making sustainable progress in this competition unless the rules are changed.

CALCULATION OF THE CHAMPIONS LEAGUE EFFECT

Bert Kassies from the Netherlands keeps a database of all matches of the clubs in the UEFA Cups as from 1959. Based on that information, the scores of the big and small countries were calculated for the period 1959–2018.[1] The big countries are Germany, France, England, Spain, and Italy. The small countries are the Netherlands, Belgium, Scotland, Hungary, Sweden, and Portugal. The small nations have strong country teams, a football culture, and many clubs with long traditions. What is particularly striking in the calculations is that although the big countries were always in the top echelons of club football, they did not completely dominate the UEFA rankings and club football. There was room for teams from smaller leagues to compete. The clubs from the small countries regularly achieved high scores. They finished high in the country rankings because they had several high-performing teams that did well internationally. English clubs did not take part in the European competitions between 1985 and 1990 because they were banned from competing after the Heysel disaster of 1985.

Miracles happen on rare occasions, but circumstances revert to normal in the following year. The distribution of funds (mainly television broadcasting rights, but large advertisers are also more interested in the winners than in the losers) leads to a winner-takes-all scenario, in which a few clubs and leagues develop into superstars. As a result, they receive extra money every year and with every new Champions League competition, thus perpetuating their lead. Only mismanagement can bring these teams to their knees. But it has turned out that even in the case of malpractice (doping, match-fixing, and so forth) big clubs have no problems in sweeping it under the carpet. After all, the big international federations and supervisory bodies are mainly populated with pawns from the big clubs. The cliquish mentality guarantees that nothing much will change.

With their enormous financial resources, big clubs preventively buy as much talent as possible, preferably from small clubs and/or small leagues. Sometimes that talent does not even play on the new team but is simply left with the selling club and rented out. It is crazy how large football clubs even buy entire teams in order to have all that football talent play within their sphere of influence. The fact that the football regulators allow this to happen is indicative of a large degree of what can be called (for want of a better word) a blurring of standards. The

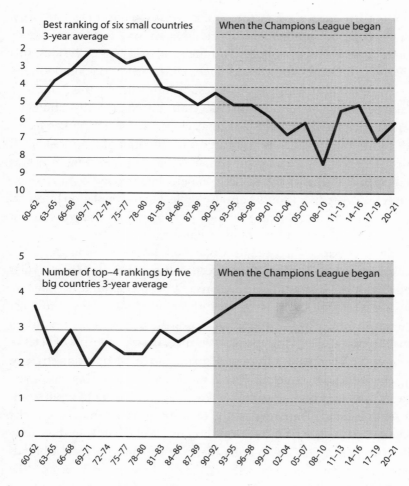

Figure 4.1   The Champions League effect: Small countries do not score anymore
Source: Bert Kassies's database.

small clubs may be happy with the large sums of money paid for their young players but fail to realize that they are destined to remain obscure forever. The system is self-perpetuating. The big teams have bought so many talented players that their B team can easily become champions in a small football league. This narrows the options for those small leagues: accept this reality or build a bigger league and then make the jump. This is another component that is vital to the Champions League effect: big encourages even more big.

I am painting a stark picture, but this has the advantage of clarity. Many people are familiar with sports competitions, and the metaphor makes it easy to better understand the economic game. Besides, this effect is sufficiently known and documented in sports competitions across different disciplines. As a result, for example, the American National Basketball Association (NBA) introduced corrective strategies to rebalance small and large basketball clubs. The lowest-ranked teams are allowed first choice in drafting from the pool of new basketball talent. Consequently, NBA competitions remain more exciting, and fans and players of smaller teams can compete on an equal footing. These correction systems, of course, are also subject to manipulation by sports bosses: they often deliberately let their club lose for several years so that they can be the first to buy young talent at some point.

There is a parallel between the Champions League effect in sports and the real economy. The long-term effects of the Champions League rules should not be underestimated and are a fitting metaphor for gigantism. Buying up young talent from potentially competitive teams mirrors the way in which large corporations acquire fast-growing or promising small companies. Driving up takeover prices is a separate line of defence because it prevents SMEs from participating in this acquisition strategy. Big sponsors go to big clubs, just as big governments or big customers like to work with big companies. It is a new entry barrier to small teams in small leagues. Translated to the business world, Amazon is in the Champions League, and the local shop or small chain is in the Croky (Belgian) League. It is almost ironic that multinationals use their A-brands in the Champions League and their B-brands in local competitions. The positions are self-perpetuating, and the gap between small and large players expands with each new start of the football competition. Unless the rules for the competition are changed, this will simply continue.

The big countries have gained an unbridgeable advantage through the Champions League effect. Television rights, sponsorship contracts, subscription fees, and money from city-trip tourism – everything has become bigger for the current top clubs such as Barcelona, Manchester, Munchen, Liverpool, or Arsenal, who used to be inferior to their rivals from smaller countries, such as Ajax, Anderlecht, Porto, Celtic Glasgow, or Steaua Bucharest. The income of the twenty clubs of the Premier League, the highest English football league, is greater than that of the

597 top clubs in all forty-eight European football countries *together*, excluding Germany, France, Spain, Turkey, and Russia. Yet there are countries in those leagues – think of the Netherlands, Portugal, Belgium, Sweden, and Scotland – that used to raise top European clubs. The chance of a top team (one capable of competing for years with the big countries' teams) emerging again from these small leagues is almost zero at the moment. That has nothing to do with their young talent, the enthusiasm of their supporters, or the will of their club management but everything to do with the rules of the European competition.[2]

The Champions League effect establishes a neat link between cause (the rules of the game) and effect (big clubs becoming bigger, the small ones smaller). In the same way, the rules of the game in the real economy, described in the previous chapter, stimulate consequences, consequences that are farther reaching than merely the dividing line between large and small. The example of the Champions League also makes clear that there is a difference between the effects after one round and the effects after several rounds or between the short term and the long term. The reformers of Europe's UEFA competitions probably never intended to dwarf small countries and small clubs in the long run; they wanted an exciting top league with top players and top clubs. Only after three to five years did it first become clear that there were also unintended ramifications. So far, everything indicates that the effect will only become worse, and the gap will become wider. The big clubs appear to be working on their own super league, a private league. The eleven founding clubs would have a place in this super league for twenty years.[3] Five other clubs would be allowed to participate as "guests."[4] If these plans become a reality, gigantism will become engrained in football. It would kill some of the excitement in the sport. The "small" family clubs and the unpredictable aspects (that Leicester City would become champion of the English football league, for example) would cease to exist. With gigantism, the soul, the humanity, of the sport dies.

The fact that, after more than twenty-five years of the Champions League, the European competition is not being reformed may have everything to do with the lobbying of the big clubs and the big competitions. As soon as a situation becomes serious, it becomes difficult to change, and reforms from the top are guaranteed to fail if the top is known to have been appointed by the main beneficiaries.

Gigantic Constructions

Encouraging gigantism ultimately has an impact on the way our cities and buildings develop, as well as on machines and organizational forms. The Champions League effect is ubiquitous.

In shipping, a league of super-ports is under formation, in Singapore, Shanghai, Busan (South Korea), Dubai, Hong Kong, and Rotterdam. Such ports encourage the use of mammoth container ships, which can only berth in deep-water ports. By doing so, they create an entry barrier and downgrade the other ports.

The same mechanism is at play in aviation, in which some airports are assigned hub status and become major nodes: Atlanta, London, Dubai, Singapore, Chicago, or Frankfurt airport. Super-sized aircraft such as the Airbus A380 can land and take off there. Other airports become spokes or feeder airports, no longer able to offer travellers the direct connections to major world cities they once had.

In this way, cities are also pushed into the Champions League effect: positions are allocated and entry barriers are erected, preventing newcomers and latecomers from entering the top tier. Critical readers will no doubt argue that this trend offers multiple advantages. Big cities, huge harbours, and mammoth airports are more efficient, aren't they? Surely XL-sized vessels and aircraft are incredible machines that promote efficiency? This is undoubtedly true, but the disadvantages and long-term effects should not be overlooked. They promote a certain model, while, in principle, other models could be equally possible.

This is what I want to make clear with this book; if we make adjustments, we can encourage other economic models. Gauged according to certain criteria, they may seem less efficient in the short term but are infinitely more sustainable and gain in efficiency if one broadens the horizon.

Buildings offer another good example of gigantism. Whether they are large government campuses (the European Union, the European Central Bank, the Pentagon, the structure that houses the Communist Party of China) or the headquarters of enormous companies, their role is to signal to the outside world the values that are enshrined within: power, prestige, inviolability (take your pick).

I was able to visit Apple's new company building in Cupertino, California (see figure 4.2), and had a meeting with management. The

Figure 4.2 Apple headquarters in Cupertino, California

"spaceship," as Apple's headquarters are called, has a circumference of 1.6 kilometres (1.0 mile) and a diameter of 500 metres. It has four floors. A gem of engineering, it is super-efficient, especially in terms of energy use. The roof is covered with solar panels, and the building needs only 30 per cent additional energy for its needs. Yet the building is so clean, so pure, so white that it seems sterile. I hesitated to step inside wearing shoes soiled by the path around the building. Like everything else in the structure – the chairs, the coffee stations, the meeting rooms – the glass is spotless. One cannot help feeling that the spaceship was designed for Apple robots rather than people. It is an impressive architectural specimen, similar in that regard to the Basilica of Saint Peter in Vatican City; it has little to do with people, and everything to do with the status of the organization at the time it was built. The spaceship emanates the power of Apple, a company that at the time had USD 250 billion in cash on its balance sheet and for which the estimated USD 4 billion to USD 5 billion in construction costs were a drop in the financial ocean. I wonder who will be in that complex in fifty years' time. After all, technology companies tend not to live forever. Even former tech giants such as IBM struggle to hold onto their position after a few decades. Apple's headquarters is one of the most colossal corporate buildings in the world. If the company is surpassed in prestige or megalomania in the short term, you can bet on Google, Amazon, Alibaba, or another Tencent being the champion.

I cannot imagine that the 828 metre high Burj Khalifa in Dubai, United Arab Emirates, was built with the motto "Let's create a pleasant building for the local people." The world's tallest tower was designed as the embodiment of the power and prestige of the UAE and as a statement to other countries that once boasted the highest building in the world: Taiwan, Malaysia, and the United States. Projects such as these are not about people but about the power of a country or an organization. Gigantism serves power, not people.

Big Beers, Fewer Flavours

The trend towards increasing size can also be illustrated in a sector that we Belgians know well: beer. The tradition of beer brewing has cultural and even religious roots. Beer has been produced for thousands of years, but the ancient Romans preferred wine; those peoples who were dubbed "uncivilized" specialized in beer. As early as 98 CE, the Roman consul, historian, writer, and orator Publius Cornelius Tacitus described how the Germans, whom he deemed "lazy," brewed an alcoholic drink based on barley and rye. They also drank "too much beer," he noted. The monks refined the process and added hops, which improved the taste and the shelf life.

Belgian beer production has been refined, and techniques and recipes passed down over the centuries. Each village had its own brewery or breweries. Abbeys made cheese and beer and were also interested in what we refer to today as research and development, and innovation: different flavours, strengths, and packaging. It was in this biotope that, from the twentieth century onwards, some breweries embarked on the *integration of a fragmented sector*. Piedbœuf, until then a very small local brewer, bought a string of breweries and consolidated them into a group. The brewery Artois did likewise at around the same time and under its umbrella launched brands such as Stella, Hoegaarden, and Wielemans. In 1988 the two merged to form Interbrew, becoming a large Belgian beer group. It did not stop there, however. In 2004 the merger with

Figure 4.3   No small beer: The formation of beer giant AB InBev

Brazilian company AmBev marked a gigantic leap forward. In 2008 falling interest rates and the rationalization of its beer group enabled AmBev to take over the American giant Anheuser-Busch. When the debts had subsided and interest rates took another dive, in 2015 the Belgians were able to make a play for SABMiller, originally a South African concern (see figure 4.3). With these takeovers, AB InBev group now owns 30 per cent of today's global beer market.

AB InBev and its shareholders have built an incredible empire. They followed the rules and seized whatever opportunities they could. In every respect they are an example of how gigantism is facilitated by macro-conditions: falling interest rates, different tax rates for large and small companies, globalization, and so on. It is a business and financial success for large and small shareholders alike. But the story does not end there. The broader consequences are less publicized but at least as far reaching. In the last few decades diverse local beers and special flavours and varieties have disappeared. With the beers, the traditions and local breweries that supported local initiatives have also disappeared. Students used to drink Jack-Op but are now content to quaff Jupiler or Stella. Many artisanal beers went under; their market was swallowed up by the larger beers. Sometimes production was relocated, though not always without a struggle.

This struggle became painfully clear when AB InBev tried to move the production of the "blond" beer Hoegaarden from the village of the same name to Liège in 2005. In the end it was not the protests that caused the plan to collapse but the altered taste and colour of the beer. In 2007, production returned to the beer's home region of Hageland.

The villages lost their local brewery, their special beer, their cherished brew, and their own café, where townspeople met after every party, funeral, and hard day's work. Now we all drink the same industrial beer, hardly ever in picturesque, quirky village pubs and usually in chain restaurants or cafés that are now all dependent on that one big brewer, with the same decor, the same signboard, and the same selection of beer and other beverages. In the beer market, gigantism is responsible for the disappearance of many local beers. The Belgian brands Stella and Leffe are now drunk worldwide. Unfortunately Belgian beer culture itself has become vastly impoverished.

This concept of eliminating potential competitors through acquisition has a name: killer acquisition.[5] Enterprises are encouraged to buy innovative prey to prevent them developing the projects that could turn them into future rivals. Remember the buying of promising footballers in our Champions League story?

At company level, researchers looked for and found substantial evidence of killer acquisitions.[6] They analyzed 35,000 projects involving pharmaceutical products developed by large and small companies. The products of the pharmaceutical companies that were acquired were less likely to be developed further if there was an overlap with the buyer's product portfolio. This was especially the case if the buyer had a strong market position in that area. The researchers concluded that 6.4 per cent of all acquisitions (or more than 2,000 projects) were killer acquisitions. The antitrust authorities failed to notice them because at the time they were too small to be reported or spotted. Such acquisitions are one of the reasons that giants stifle innovation and cause overpricing.

Mainstream Taste Is Your Taste

In the food sector, too, a small number of large companies determine which raw materials are used, what is put on the shelves, and what eventually ends up on your plate. Monsanto (which has now become part of Bayer) accounts for 85 per cent of the American grain market and 91 per cent of the soybean market. This has had an impact on agriculture and has even pushed small farmers out of the market in the United States. If we move on to the manufactured foods, other big players appear. Oxfam charted this phenomenon in an impressive diagram (see figure 4.4). The ten food giants are Associated British Foods (ABF), Coca-Cola, Danone, General Mills, Kellogg's, Mars, Mondelez, Nestlé, PepsiCo, and Unilever. The brands they have in their portfolio are often better known than the giant's own name, and most consumers are probably unaware that they are part of a group. These ten groups account for 47 per cent of the fast-food market.

Within certain segments their dominance is even greater. Fifty-eight per cent of potato chips are marketed by the Lay's brand, which is owned by the American multinational PepsiCo. The Gatorade label accounts for 75 per cent of sports drinks in the United States and is also owned by PepsiCo. To give a final example, the American group Mars controls 15 per cent of the global chocolate market, but 40 per cent of the Chinese market and even 48 per cent of the Indian market.

Large food companies focus heavily on the consumer's desire for safety: if a product is made by a large entity, it must be okay. If you want to eat something abroad and have little faith in the local cuisine, the fast food chain McDonald's is the beacon you aim for.

Not that there are no positive arguments to be made. Unilever, for example, has an inspiring-purpose strategy and wants to bring people healthy food. That is wonderful, but the point I want to make is that a whole host of smaller food companies want to do the same but simply cannot get into the supermarket. Our taste is literally and figuratively determined by a limited number of food giants. To make it as easy as possible for us, companies are looking for our sweet spot. That can be taken literally too: our food products contain far more sugar than is good for us because we are more likely to eat sugary foods than others. Our eating habits have been derailed, landing us in a global epidemic of obesity, which in turn triggers other health problems, such as diabetes. Of course, there is a pharmaceutical product for every health issue (see figure 4.4).

If one craves unique flavours, one must venture further than the supermarket and discover them in farmers' markets and independent shops, or provided by individuals or restaurants that still practise the art of small pleasures. Our tastes are becoming mainstream, supply is shrinking, and *one size fits all* is increasingly the norm on a global scale.

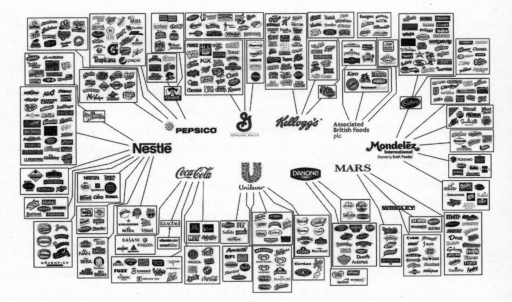

Figure 4.4   Know what you are eating: The giants of the food industry

Sources: Oxfam; also see Oxfam International, "Behind the Brands," 26 February 2013, https://www.oxfam.org/en/research/behind-brands.

The Walmart-ization of Retail and the Economy

The American concern Walmart is the largest supermarket chain in the world and one of the world's largest companies. Every member of the Walton family ranks among the list of America's ultra-rich. The company employs 2.2 million people, 1.5 million of whom work in the United States alone. Walmart has more than 10,000 retail outlets and accounts for 25 per cent of all retail in the United States. More than half of the products on the shelves come from China. The combined surface area of all Walmart stores is roughly one and a half times that of Manhattan. Ninety per cent of all Americans live within a twenty-four-kilometre radius of a Walmart.

Walmart's unprecedented expansion was driven by a blend of audacity, business acumen, and the growth factors outlined in chapter 2. In Europe, Walmart is relatively unknown, but replace Walmart with Ikea or Decathlon, and the parallels persist. One of the arguments against throwing obstacles in the path of these giants is the employment they create. Each time a factory closes somewhere in Europe, causing significant job losses, people welcome the arrival of a Decathlon or an Ikea "because they bring a lot of jobs." Job creation is a first-round effect of opening a large store. Yet it pays to examine the long-term consequences of gigantism in the retail sector.

Bill de Blasio, the mayor of New York City from 2014 to 2021, commissioned a study in 2012 on the effects of the Walmart department store group on local communities. That led to the report *Walmart's Economic Footprint*, with a comprehensive overview of fifty scientific studies on the economic impact of the retailer on the entire American economy. With this report the City of New York wanted to be able to make informed decisions about new Walmart locations. The main conclusion of the report was that every new Walmart in New York City would destroy more jobs than it would create. The disappearance of numerous independent shops would also ultimately increase the tax burden. The mayor said, "The history of the last decade tells us that Wal-Mart stands to be our City's [New York's] Trojan Horse."[7] He was talking not only about the closure of small shops but also about the low wages because Walmart pays its employees a salary that is barely above the minimum wage.

The studies on Walmart provide a fantastic insight into the Champions League effect, as they juxtapose the short-term consequences and the long-term consequences. In the short term, employment and the purchasing power of the local population increase as a result of the arrival of cheap products. However, the adverse effects do not make themselves felt for several years, in the form of net job losses and new jobs that are poorly paid. The result is a decline in the overall economy. Walmart does not deny that its staff earns very little and barely makes ends meet. A spokesperson said: "More than two-thirds of our people … are not trying to support a family. That's who our jobs are designed for."[8] I do not know whether we should catalogue this under irony, sarcasm, or utter lack of feeling.

What these studies do not measure is the broader socio-economic impact of the arrival of such a large retail shop. The entire logistical process will change: local purchases will drop off entirely in favour of international purchases; consumers will travel predominantly by car; other local shops will attract fewer customers because people will no longer shop in the centre of the city but in enormous retail centres on the outskirts. Unlike independent shopkeepers, Walmart staff do not feel as connected with customers, and treat them in a routine fashion. Customers increasingly adopt the role of shop assistant, seeking out products and their availability, making their own choices, scanning their purchases, and paying for them with their bank card at a self-service station; then they load the goods into their car in the car park. The entire experience of shopping locally is thus transformed into a fairly standardized, industrial shopping experience, where efficiency and profitability are paramount. Before long, alternative retail options vanish, too, so that the giant supermarkets are able to expand their market share. Standardization supplants human interaction, communities unravel, and wages and products become junk. No, I am not a fan of the Walmart-ization of the economy.

E-commerce has changed this form of retail to some extent but not completely. The Internet economy displays the same characteristics of gigantism and has the same consequences for consumers and employment. The working conditions at American e-commerce company Amazon or German online fashion retailer Zalando are no different from those at Walmart; delivery-van jockeys must drop off packages for starvation wages, and the consumer is inundated with junk, brought in from the four corners of the world. The ecological footprint of this form of retail is enormous and causes great damage to the environment. Now the old retail giants are being squeezed by even bigger, young, swiftly growing, new retail giants. The former are vulnerable to innovation and rapid change, lulled into complacency by their decades-long untouchable status.

Big Pharma: Diseases Are Big Business

The global pharmaceutical market is worth an estimated USD 1,400 billion. North America, Asia, and Western Europe account for almost 80 per cent of the drug market. The ten largest pharmaceutical companies take some 40 per cent of the market, the top fifteen more than 50 per cent (see figure 4.5). Big pharma therefore sets the rules. This sector is also in thrall to gigantism.

On the one hand, pharmaceuticals is an industry in which size is essential to secure adequate resources for research and development and

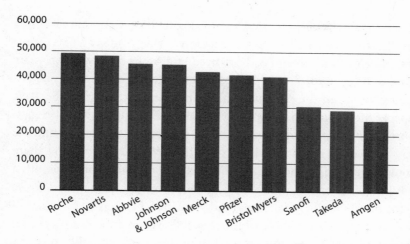

Figure 4.5   How big pharma controls the pharmaceuticals market: Turnover in USD millions

The top 10 pharma companies account for 40% of the market, the top 15 for more than 50% of the market.

Sources: 2021 annual reports.

for building a global sales network. On the other hand, mergers have substantially increased concentration in the industry, and it is a sector in which the big players define the market. For these corporations the government is a vital factor, determining many of the ground rules for drug approvals and, later, reimbursements. Unsurprisingly, the powerful pharmaceutical manufacturers go to great lengths to influence the government. Figures from the independent research firm Center for Responsive Politics reveal that the American pharmaceutical sector has some two lobbyists for each member of the US Congress.

Through all manner of mergers and acquisitions the American company Pfizer has evolved into the world leader in medicines. Pfizer is primarily known for products such as Viagra, although Lipitor (anti-cholesterol) and Xanax (antidepressant) are also blockbuster drugs. Pfizer was founded in 1849 but saw rapid growth after the turn of the millennium through a series of acquisitions including Warner-Lambert, Wyeth, Pharmacia, and Hospira. It is a true giant, harnessing the factors set out in the second chapter. Pfizer can borrow in euros at 0.3 per cent interest. This provides enormous leverage for acquisitions, share buy-backs, or other capital operations. Money is practically free for the pharmaceutical company. I have absolutely no intention of singling out Pfizer here; after all, the same situation applies to many giants. Apple and Microsoft, for example, borrowed at 0.9 per cent over ten years around the year 2020. For all giants, then, money was almost free.

Gigantism in the pharmaceutical industry certainly has positive aspects: more research resources to develop new drugs, more efficiency, more opportunities for patients to buy cheaper drugs, and so on. The COVID-19 crisis has also demonstrated this. Without big pharma, there would have been no vaccine. Although, again, it should not be forgotten that BioNTech and Crucell were smaller players, playing a crucial role in the development of vaccines, and were incorporated by big pharma or drawn into their sphere of influence. Governments also played an important role, providing funding to big pharma. In addition to the admiration for the relatively rapid and frequent development of vaccines, there was also a great deal of criticism of the big pharma companies. However, this did not yield them extreme share price gains. AstraZeneca and Johnson & Johnson performed well below the stock markets during the COVID-19 period – due to a number of specific issues but also to the fact that there were strict agreements with the governments regarding price and purchasing.

The evolution of concentration within the pharmaceutical sector goes hand in hand with a worldwide overconsumption of medicines. The use of painkillers, sedatives, antidepressants, anxiety inhibitors, ADHD medication, anti-cholesterol drugs, and Viagra has increased and become so prevalent that one can speak of drug dependency. It is curious that addiction to drugs is not considered a reason for the US Food and Drug Administration to block the entrance of a pharma product. When dealing with health issues, chemistry is becoming a substitute for natural healing processes. Many of us are completely out of balance and rely on pharmaceuticals to regain an artificial equilibrium. Gigantism exacerbates this problem: the pharmaceutical companies are so powerful that their tentacles extend into controlling and advisory bodies. The West has a prescription addiction, and big pharma certainly will not object to that.

There is no denying the fact that many people who take prescription drugs do so for a prolonged period of time. In the United States, 60 per cent of users take antidepressants for at least two years; 14 per cent even

Figure 4.6   The use of antidepressants is depressing

Source: OECD Health Statistics 2021.

take them for ten years or more. Worldwide, the use of antidepressants is on the rise (see figure 4.6). There is no correlation, for example, between a country's happiness index and drug consumption use. In some cases, consumption in affluent countries is high, yet very low in others. Nor is there a clear correlation with suicide. The differences are multi-layered and related to prescription behaviour, therapeutic practices, and many other issues. In America more than 10 per cent of the population take antidepressants. The United States is a major consumer of a broad array of pharmaceuticals, including painkillers: having 4 per cent of the world's population, America consumes more than 30 per cent of all painkillers.

To say that big pharma is the root of drug overconsumption may be an exaggeration, although the large pharmaceutical companies are obviously not complaining about the uptick in long-term drug use. Sleeping pills, painkillers, tranquillizers, and antidepressants have become everyday commodities; the threshold to obtaining them is very low. Moreover, some drugs are addictive or mood-enhancing: over time the body may develop a tolerance and require ever-increasing doses to achieve the same effect. In other cases, drugs must be used in combination to maintain a day-and-night rhythm. The role of big pharma warrants scrutiny; what is at issue is not simply our health but a miscellany of serious social issues. It is a topic that merits further debate and is a direct outgrowth of gigantism.

In fact, gigantism breeds dehumanization. We are drifting further and further away from human solutions and closer to industrialized, mass-produced, standardized remedies. The structural solution to depression or obesity is not better chemistry but better chemistry between people, their natural environment, their workplace, and society. In a success-oriented society many of us struggle to cope in the rat race and rely on sleeping pills and painkillers to manage stress and other symptoms. Medications can offer a stimulus but should not become ingrained, otherwise the consumption of pharmaceutical products will come to resemble that of electricity and energy: an ever-present, recurring bill that people must pay to continue participating in society.

Big Tech: Each Has Its Own Monopoly

As indicated earlier in this book, the situation became unmanageable when, despite many legal battles and legal proceedings in the 1990s, Microsoft, the software company of Bill Gates and the late Paul Allen, was not broken up. This set a precedent for subsequent technology giants. It would have been far better if Microsoft had been split into, say, a company for PC operating systems, a company for the development

Figure 4.7   Tech giants and their satellite companies

of word processing and spreadsheets software, and a young but growing business branch for Internet browsers. This did not happen, and today other technology giants can follow suit: they can concentrate multiple activities and take over potential competitors at an early stage.

The big tech giants would rather avoid direct confrontation. This creates large conglomerates which, through countless takeovers, are becoming increasingly dominant in their "niche." Microsoft, Facebook, Google, Amazon, and Apple are hardly rivals; each has built up its own empire, which may carry the label "technology" but has little in common with the empires of the other IT giants (see figure 4.7). While Microsoft has carved out a comfortable position in corporate environments, Amazon specializes in retail and cloud services. While Facebook is the dominant player in social media, Google increasingly focuses on artificial intelligence and the like. Finally, Apple feels more at home in consumer products and – with the exception of a few Microsoft products, Google operating systems, and the Chinese counterparts in their market – faces virtually no competition from the other tech giants. In this manner, near-monopolies or oligopolies in the worst case have emerged, and the barriers to entry by potential competitors have soared to the dizzy heights of the Burj Khalifa.

Conclusion

"Hotel California," the famous song by the American band the Eagles, is about a place from which you can check out at any time, but you can never leave. In "Hotel Champions League" you can turn up whenever you like, but you will never get in. Every room is occupied, and the guests are going from strength to strength and will not leave of their own accord. Meanwhile the hotel manager has become their bosom buddy. Those who cannot get a room are left out in the cold, and the temperature outside is falling with frightening rapidity. The hotel only has room for a limited number of guests in an equally limited number of rooms. The price of admission increases by the year, and the amenities just keep getting better. What is more, the hotels in the area are being driven out of the market and forced to further reduce their capacity and services.

The Champions League has delivered great football performance but at the same time has industrialized football. The top European league has cultivated tourist supporters at major clubs such as Barcelona, Manchester, or Liverpool, but the real football fan, who has remained true to his traditional club, has often been left out in the cold. Even dyed-in-the-wool supporters are crowded out of the stadium because the VIP packages are more lucrative than the terraces. Die-hard fans of small traditional clubs are left with nothing to look forward to because young players are bought at the first sign of real talent. Major sponsors no longer come to watch these small teams, choosing instead to pool their national budgets to offer a megabudget to that one European Champions League club.

Today, we see the emergence of a Champions League in numerous sectors: food, beer, technology, consultancy, logistics, derivatives, pharmaceuticals, car tires, credit rating, film, or toothpaste. A Champions League is a de facto oligopoly but is not always considered as such. Of course, a major league of this stature does offer advantages, such as top quality, but it also has disadvantages: less or slower truly ground-breaking innovation and less competition. In addition, a Champions League may have effects beyond the purely economic, as I explained in the case of food, beer, and pharmaceuticals. A Champions League will deliver more industrialized products and services at the expense of community cohesion and people-related products and services. In the worst-case scenario, the trend leads to the dehumanization of the economy. That should indeed be worrying to all of us.

GIGANTISM DISRUPTS SOCIETY

In the previous chapter the metaphor of sports was used to illustrate how gigantism has spread across various sectors. I also touched on the economic impact of gigantism: concentration, lack of competition, barriers to entry, and changes in social behaviour. This chapter offers a detailed analysis of the repercussions for the individual human being. A number of key trends, that are called diseases of affluence, such as social inequality and crime, are related to gigantism. I will also revisit a number of important examples from the previous chapters, but from a different perspective. This time, the human being is pitted against the giant – personalism as a counterweight to unbalanced fake capitalism.

Walmart-ization Leads to Obesity

Retail is probably the sector that has been affected the longest by economies of scale. The rise of supermarkets dates to the golden sixties, more than half a century ago. The consequences have since been extensively researched by scientists and economists.

In the United States, 1962 saw the birth of gigantism in the retail sector: the opening of the first Walmart, Target, and Kmart big boxes. The emergence of this retail format had a profound impact on the local community. It moved shopping out of the city centre to the outskirts, and because the big boxes were not within walking distance, one needed a car. The stores were not run by families that everyone had known for generations, but by managers, often brought in from places much further away. The stores were many times larger than a small, local shop and had large retail facilities, giant car parks, and an enormous selection of merchandise, mostly on sale for highly discounted prices. Since 1962,

Walmart supermarkets in the United States have multiplied from one to forty-six hundred. In the meantime the other megaretailers (Target and Kmart) have more than a thousand stores each, joined by a host of new, large chain stores.[1] Later on, another trend appeared on the scene, the shopping centre, a retail concept combining big department stores with smaller-scale boutiques – gigantic entities when taken as a whole.

In recent years e-commerce has delivered several body blows to this form of megaretail, although it continues to dominate. For example, Walmart employs almost 1 per cent of the total labour force in the United States;[2] it is the country's largest importer, with 900,000 containers per year,[3] and 70 to 80 per cent of these goods come from China.[4] The massive proliferation of supermarkets and shopping centres has obviously had a major impact on employment. A study conducted by the Massachusetts Institute of Technology in 2008 shows that supermarkets have eradicated half of the jobs in the mom-and-pop stores, the small, independent businesses that are family-owned.[5] Other studies show that when a megastore opens somewhere, an average of fourteen smaller shops in the neighborhood go out of business in the next twelve months.

The social impact does not stop there, however. In 2011, Professor Charles Courtemanche of the University of Kentucky concluded that there is a direct link between the emergence of hypermarkets and the increase in obesity.[6] He found that each additional supercentre increases an area's body mass index (BMI) by 0.24 units and the obesity rate by 2.3 percentage points. That may seem trivial, but the opposite is true: it means that the proliferation of Walmart hypermarkets alone is responsible for the 10.5 per cent uptick in obesity since the late 1980s. Walmart's sale of cheap goods, which can be considered a positive outcome, is insufficient to compensate for the increase in health expenditure. This means that if you look at Walmart-ization narrowly, you focus only on lower costs. But when you look at the big picture, you see that Walmart-ization negatively affects the economy; in short, it diminishes prosperity. Although they are now thoroughly documented, the profound social repercussions of gigantism in the retail sector are not widely known. In the United States, the crime rate spiked when local shops in communities disappeared.[7] This is easily verifiable if one compares towns with and without Walmart megastores. Studies found that employment rates and tax revenues declined in areas where Walmart expanded.

In view of this, it is astonishing that political leaders continue to approve the establishment of gigantic Walmart-style retail centres in the

United States, or Ikea and Decathlon in Europe. I am not suggesting that every Decathlon or Ikea is bad or that they bring no positive effects. One can argue that Decathlon encourages a large segment of the population to become involved in sports. The question is, however, whether we have given sufficient thought to the negative impact of the entry of such titans. If we have, we might ask why the government continues to create incentives or provide direct grants to these massive retail companies at the minute they float a balloon indicating they are considering an investment plan. Think of sites that can be bought for a pittance or the access roads that the state is happy to build for them. To manipulate public opinion, massive shopping centres are even marketed as a *job strategy*, despite a lack of economic research to back this up. Not all aspects are taken into account, and long-term effects are not factored in (see chapter 4).

Again, I do not say that big retail brings no advantages. Large supermarkets have vastly increased consumer choice, while prices for that same consumer have fallen. Management positions, unnecessary in small, independent shops, have also been created in the sector. But these advantages are not sufficiently offset by the socio-economic disadvantages, which usually only manifest after a longer period of time. The decline of small shops is gradual and goes almost unnoticed, unlike the closure of a factory or the bankruptcy of a large chain.

What is more, it is absurd that each time a large factory closes its doors, politicians wave subsidies around to attract a large franchise, or, when a shopping centre opens, they have only praise for the "new employment project." This is not simply counterproductive; it is wrong to believe that jobs in retail have the same leverage effect on job creation in other (supply) sectors. The leverage of manufacturing sectors (such as industry and software) are manifoldly greater than that of retail, logistics, and distribution. A country becomes impoverished when its manufacturing sectors disappear; a population becomes impoverished when it gives more room to consumption than to creation.

The Disappearing Middle Class

The link between employment and gigantism is abundantly clear in the department store sector. This can also be extended to several other sectors, such as the hospitality industry and other local activities. However, it is much more difficult to establish other causal links with absolute certainty. For some time the impact of automation on employment has been the subject of debate. Some say that automation will not displace a vast number of jobs, but a question that is rarely answered or even researched is the impact on society when people's working lives are disrupted. Economists are quick to claim that automation makes "stupid jobs" disappear, paving the way for the creation of "more rewarding jobs."

That is one possible scenario, but it also misses the crux of the matters: jobs serve both a social *and* an economic function. Small shops may not be "as economically valuable," but they fulfill a social role. Buying fruit and vegetables from a local grocer, with all the personal contact this entails – not only with the shopkeeper but also with other customers – is an entirely different experience to buying the same or similar products at a supermarket. Our social fabric is made up of personal contact and encounters. It creates a sense of connection and a better understanding of one another. Megastores are less interested in these interactions and are more focused on transactions. Unfortunately, the overlap between economy and society is not a popular domain of research. Neither is an exact science, which can sometimes lead to conflicting opinions or research results.

The analysis I present here is based partly on statistics and thorough research and also, to some extent, on a personal interpretation. While it is fairly easy to substantiate gigantism economically, it has never been a field of research in the social domain. Nevertheless, gigantism must be considered in light of the important social phenomena that concern us today: inequality, social mobility, diseases of affluence (such as burnout, depression, and obesity), entrepreneurship, diversity, and so on.

Another important social phenomenon is the polarization of jobs and the pressure on the middle class – some even speak of the disappearance of the middle class. Researchers Maarten Goos, Alan Manning, and Anna Salomons have shown that the labour market in Europe is polarizing.[8] This means, on the one hand, that there is an increase in the number of low-paying jobs, while, on the other hand, the number of high-paying jobs is rising. As a result, the middle class is shrinking in all countries (see figure 5.1).

Optimists will declare that the middle class has never had it "so good" and is becoming richer, but the polarization of the labour market is a picture that is emerging in almost all European countries. Highly qualified jobs pay better than low-skilled jobs. The well-paid middle class

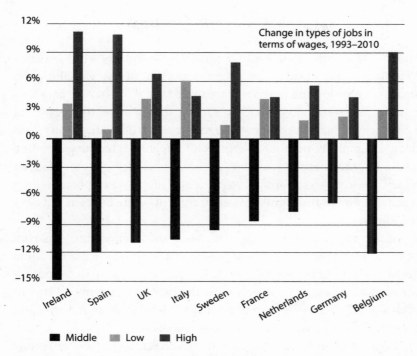

Figure 5.1   The disappearing middle class: Evolution of high- versus low- and medium-paying jobs in Europe

Source: Goos, Manning, and Salomons, "Explaining Job Polarization."

is under pressure, and the war for talent is being increasingly fought over the best educated, who then progress into high-earning positions.

The pressure on the middle class is also a concern in the United States. After all, inequality in America is more acute because of taxation and the lack of extensive transfers (as they are known in Europe). The researchers who investigated polarization found three main causes: globalization, delocalization, and technological changes. The latter is often referred to as "the demise of routine-based jobs." Today small-scale companies are still less automated than large corporations. Automation often requires some form of standardization of tasks, which is easier for large companies, thanks to the scale of their operations. So, one can certainly argue whether gigantism is at the heart of the vanishing middle class, although it would appear, at the very least, that both phenomena share the same origins.

Diseases of Affluence

I have already noted that researchers have demonstrated a link between Walmart-ization and obesity. Other important diseases of affluence, such as depression and burnout, have soared lately and have equal social relevance. It seems no coincidence to me that, parallel to a period of rampant gigantism, the burnout rate has increased dramatically in recent decades. Employee burnout in large tech companies is reaching alarming levels. A comprehensive 2018 study on burnout caused a storm in Silicon Valley.[9] Between 50 and around 70 per cent of employees reported feeling burnt out due to the high-stress environment of the big tech industry (see figure 5.2).

Apple: 57 per cent burnout ratio. Microsoft: 57 per cent. Amazon: 59 per cent. Google: 54 per cent. Facebook: "only" 49 per cent. These are shocking figures for an industry that is on its way to becoming the ultimate example for everyone in the twenty-first century. That in itself should be enough to convince the reader that there is something thoroughly wrong with these business models.

As the number of reported burnouts for the entire (American) economy is less than 50 per cent, the figures for the tech industry certainly highlight the seriousness of the problem in that sector. Can the same be said of all megacompanies? Is it true that there are significantly more burnouts in large entities than in small companies? Unfortunately I have yet to find a large-scale study that establishes this conclusively for the entire American or European economy.

There are interesting partial studies showing that "size" has an impact on the number of burnouts. In the United States, a study on burnouts in the health sector showed that the burnout rate for doctors working in large organizations (hospitals and large medical practices) was almost 55 per cent – higher than five years earlier, when it was 45 per cent.[10] At 55 per cent, the burnout rate among physicians at large hospitals and practices matches the burnout figures in big tech. This figure is all the more alarming given that physicians are the people we rely on to understand and treat our health issues. For doctors with a private practice or active in smaller-scale environments, the percentage fell to 13. The researchers also found that the independence and autonomy associated with smaller medical practices offered protection against the symptoms of burnout.

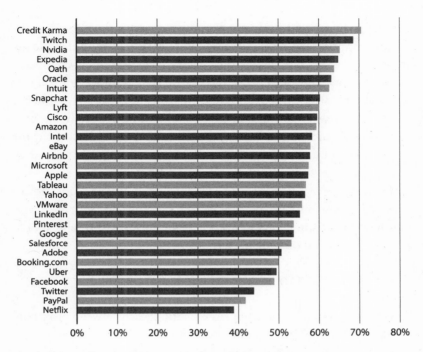

Figure 5.2 Working in a high-tech company? High risk of burnout: Burnout ratios in tech companies

Percentage of respondents who answered "yes" to the question "Are you currently suffering from burnout?"

Source: Blind, https://www.teamblind.com/blog/index.php/2018/05/29/close-to-60-percent-of-surveyed-tech-workers-are-burnt-out-credit-karma-tops-the-list-for-most-employees-suffering-from-burnout/.

This observation gets to the heart of the matter and could, in my opinion, be extended to a great many sectors, perhaps even the economy in its entirety. Burnout is a complex condition and is closely interwoven with the way we organize our economy. In my opinion, gigantism has an important part to play in the development of this disease. Unbridled growth dehumanizes corporations and institutions. They lose touch with people and utilize their human potential precisely as they would robots: functionally, measurably, and rationally, with as little emotion or personal connection as possible because that "can stand in the way of professionalism."

While all large organizations cannot be tarred with the same brush, I am nonetheless convinced that people run a much greater risk of burnout in mega-entities. In small companies or small structures the relationship between employees is, by its very nature, much closer. Employees want to feel valued, they want to feel personally connected with their work, they want to be heard, and they want to be treated as individuals, not just employees. By taking this as a starting point, the correlation between an organization's size and employee burnout is clear to see. If burnout is caused by the dehumanization of work, by the impersonalization of responsibilities and functions in a company, then there is a link between gigantism and burnout.

Hopefully, research in this area will be stepped up. In the meantime, however, burnout is increasingly prevalent, keeping pace with the proliferation of gigantism, which in itself is a cause for concern and should prompt us to err on the side of caution.

Big Government, Less Empathy

Governments have always struggled with the choice between proximity (decentralization) and efficiency or control (greater centralization). As the road network improved and transport options increased, governments became more centralized. As a result, the gap between state and citizen widened. Looking at public services, hospitals, or schools, we see precisely the same situation: the larger the organization, the less room there is for empathy. Not only that, but in the United States it appears that there are significantly more crimes committed in large schools than in small schools (see figure 5.3). School crime correlates with size; as the school expands, so does the crime rate.[11]

Not only does crime thrive at gigantic schools, but also there is a higher incidence of bullying in them than at smaller schools. Bullying is one of the most serious problems encountered by young people and could be a significant contributing factor in adolescent depression, violence, and suicide.[12] If the size of a school is found to play a role in bullying, then, by extension, children attending large schools are far more likely to be suicidal.

Large schools are economically efficient, but they do have hidden costs. You will rarely ever hear an economist draw this conclusion and make this connection. Therefore, I call for giving careful consideration to the government's urge to increase the size of all its services, and to weigh the non-economic consequences, which go beyond crime,

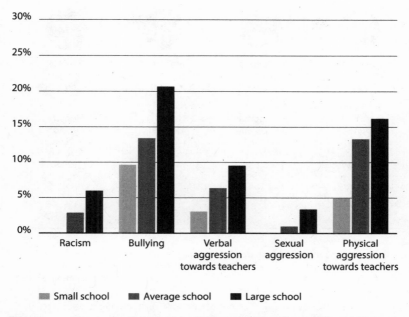

Figure 5.3 Large school, high risk of aggression: Problems with aggression in US schools, by size

Source: US Department of Education, *Digest of Education Statistics, 2020*, https://nces.ed.gov/programs/digest/.

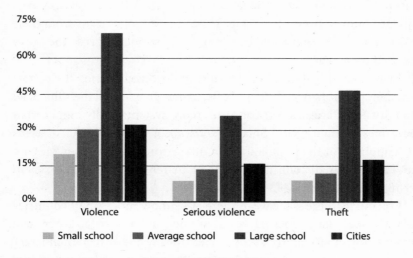

Figure 5.4 Crime and school size in the United States

Source: US Department of Education, *Digest of Education Statistics, 2020*, https://nces.ed.gov/programs/digest/2022menu_tables.asp.

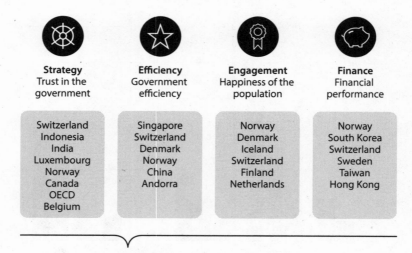

Strategy Trust in the government	Efficiency Government efficiency	Engagement Happiness of the population	Finance Financial performance
Switzerland Indonesia India Luxembourg Norway Canada OECD Belgium	Singapore Switzerland Denmark Norway China Andorra	Norway Denmark Iceland Switzerland Finland Netherlands	Norway South Korea Switzerland Sweden Taiwan Hong Kong

Small countries perform better.

• Social cohesion
• Stable democracy
• Relatively independent of larger entities

Figure 5.5   Small is beautiful – for countries, too: Best-managed countries in terms of strategy, efficiency, engagement, and finance

Source: Data based on Deloitte's "Best Managed Companies" framework.

bullying, and an increased risk of suicide. A centralized system of government also leads to alienation because the administration seems too far removed from the people. The alienation of citizens from their government is accompanied by a long-term democratic risk; today, we call that populism.

I have researched the level of quality in various countries: their strategy, their performance, the happiness of their people, and their financial stability. In all areas, small countries score systematically higher than large ones (see figure 5.5).[13] Small countries score especially well in terms of "happiness of the population"; in other words, bigger countries are not happier. Small countries also score better than large countries in terms of efficiency.

Of course, there is a caveat: there are simply more small countries than there are large ones. If we list all the elements, there are indeed reasons why small countries score systematically higher than their larger counterparts: social coherence, freedom from large entities, and a sense of belonging. These are the same elements I found in comparing large and small companies.

People like to have an accessible government, to send their children to a school where they are more than just numbers, or to use government services in the locality where they are known and invited to take part in policy and decisions. Human beings play an important role in ensuring that the economy runs smoothly and that society scores well on more than just purely economic variables.

It is no coincidence that Norway, Singapore, Switzerland, the Netherlands, Denmark, and South Korea score so highly in terms of quality. For the same reason, people prefer smaller schools and smaller hospitals to larger ones, unless, because of complications or specializations, they do not have a choice.

Megacities Crush the Individual

Cities have existed for a long time, and so have large cities. Athens is said to have had 500,000 inhabitants at its peak. Alexandria had about 300,000 in its glory days. Rome was the first city with more than one million inhabitants, half of whom were slaves. At the time, those were considered big cities, but today we would call them provincial cities. For a long time, Paris, London, New York, Tokyo, and Beijing were considered to be the very epitome of a large city. In the meantime, they, too, must tolerate many other contenders in terms of population size.

Today, in China alone, there are more than a hundred cities with more than one million inhabitants. Megacities are defined as cities with more than ten million inhabitants, and today there are at least fifty worldwide. Tokyo, Shanghai, and Jakarta are among the top three, with more than thirty million inhabitants in each. New York is just barely among the top ten (in tenth place); Paris is not even in the top thirty. Among the megacities are several cities whose names you have probably never heard of and which you could not correctly place within 500 kilometres on a blank map.

"Thirty million plus" is now the norm, but by the end of this century these cities will also dwarfed, at least if the predictions are accurate. Most of the cities forecast to be in the top twenty in 2100 will hardly ring a bell with today's readers, and even the globetrotters among us will have visited very few of them. The majority of these metropolises will no longer be in the United States, Europe, or even Asia, but in Africa (see table 5.1). In other words, Lagos, Kinshasa, Dar es Salaam, and

Table 5.1   Forecast of top 20 largest cities in the world, 2100

Ranking	City	Country	Population in 2100 (millions)
1	Lagos	Nigeria	88.3
2	Kinshasa	Congo	83.5
3	Dar Es Salaam	Tanzania	73.7
4	Mumbai	India	67.2
5	Delhi	India	57.3
6	Khartoum	Sudan	56.6
7	Niamey	Niger	56.1
8	Dhaka	Bangladesh	54.3
9	Kolkata	India	52.4
10	Khabul	Afghanistan	50.3
11	Karachi	Pakistan	49.1
12	Nairobi	Kenya	46.7
13	Lilongwe	Malawi	41.4
14	Blantyre City	Malawi	40.9
15	Cairo	Egypt	40.5
16	Kampala	Uganda	40.1
17	Manila	Philippines	40.0
18	Lusaka	Zambia	37.7
19	Mogadishu	Somalia	36.4
20	Addis Ababa	Ethiopia	35.8

Source: Global Cities Institute, *Socioeconomic Pathways*.

Mumbai – the only Asian city in the group – will become tomorrow's megacities. They are not alone, however; giant cities will become a global phenomenon by the end of this century. This is also because many leading experts see such cities as a solution to climate challenges. Per inhabitant, a city has a smaller footprint than urban sprawl has: when growth spirals out from urban centres into areas with a lower population density, the land is gobbled up by houses with big gardens, swimming pools, and other amenities.

It seems to me that the main problem is too many people, and we ought to control our demography better. But that is a taboo subject. Talking about megacities is not; it is hip. Cities are said to be efficient. They can also be automated completely, with self-driving trains, self-driving subways, self-driving buses, and self-driving cars. Yes, they are a dream for central planners, these megacities. But the big question is, Are people happy in such cities? This is a valid question because ultimately cities not only must be economically efficient but also must make the people who live in them happy. Studies on happiness and cities are rare. As has already been mentioned many times in this book, many key social issues are considered solely from an economic perspective and rarely from the dual, socio-economic dimension.

Cities offer their inhabitants many advantages. They are convenient because you will find opportunities for both service and consumption; your work is within walking distance, which may make an expensive car unnecessary; there are countless opportunities for those looking for social contact; there is plenty of culture and diversity – the list is endless. Nevertheless, cities do not usually seem to be sources of happiness, especially those cities where the density rises. Studies show that the risk of serious mental illness is higher in cities than in rural areas.[14] This is the case in both emerging and Western countries. A comprehensive Swedish study involving more than four million inhabitants concluded that mental illnesses were significantly higher in cities (the number of schizophrenia cases is even 70 per cent higher than in non-urban areas).[15] There was also a higher risk of depression – in a country that usually achieves the highest happiness scores. A study in the scientific journal *Nature* quantified mental stress in cities and concluded that the risk of schizophrenia was twice as high in an urban environment.[16] The lack of green space in cities is also associated with mental problems. A Dutch study reveals that the number of cases of depression and anxiety psychoses is significantly higher among people living in neighborhoods with only 10 per cent green space, compared to those living in neighborhoods with 90 per cent green space.[17]

The impact of mega- and gigacities on children is still inconclusive, but we need to give careful thought to how children can fully develop physically and mentally. Cities offer limited opportunities for play or participation in sports, thus hindering children's development. In a society where creativity is crucial for future employment, is an urban environment the ideal world for a new generation of creative people? Unsurprisingly, an Australian study concluded that raising young children in apartments made them sedentary.[18]

As well as the effects on children's creative development, it stands to reason that urban living multiplies the risk of obesity and associated diseases. A British study shows that 93 per cent of children living in urban high-rise apartments develop behavioral problems.[19] This figure is significantly higher in comparison to children growing up in low-rise dwellings. Social interaction is vital to happiness; living in a place where there is more social interaction is conducive to higher levels of happiness. People living in low-rise housing in rural areas have more social contact and are happier than residents of high-rise buildings in densely populated cities.[20] Other urban health problems are also gradually being identified: nearsightedness, due to a lack of depth of vision; and impaired hearing, due to exposure to noise. Add to that the fact that air quality in today's cities has deteriorated, and it is no surprise that cancer and lung diseases are more prevalent in urban hubs.

The medical journal *The Lancet* published a devastating piece on the health impact of megacities, especially in emerging markets.[21] The researchers point out poor nutrition or malnutrition, the previously mentioned risk of obesity, excessive food prices, and poverty. They also refer to studies from China and Egypt that show that there are proportionally more cases of breast cancer in cities than in rural areas. Doctors blame the large quantities of endocrine disruptors (xenoestrogens) – pesticide residues and industrial contaminants such as PCBs, dioxin, and heavy metals – that unintentionally end up in industrially produced food. The issue of urban violence is also highlighted; generally speaking, victims of violence tend to be women, who are subjected to assaults that pose a high risk of sexually transmitted diseases.

An in-depth study of the world's fifth largest city, São Paulo (Brazil), confirms this pattern of health problems. At least 30 per cent of its inhabitants suffer from mental health issues. The researchers establish a link with population density. "World population growth is projected to be concentrated in megacities," they begin.[22] This urbanisation will increase social inequality and magnify stress. "The São Paulo Metropolitan Area (SPMA) provides a forewarning of the burden of mental disorders in urban settings in [the] developing world."[23] Australian professor Tony Recsei researched urbanization and its impact on health and happiness. He concludes, as I do, that there is ample evidence confirming that people live happier and healthier lives in sparsely populated areas.[24] The gigantism that is so in vogue today attempts to convince us of the opposite. Mega- and gigacities are a dream for urban planners, certain environmental activists, and policy-makers who want a simple way to manage large masses. But human beings cannot tolerate being locked up in rabbit hutches, isolated from social contact, and treated as nothing more than a *Homo economicus*. Social interaction, freedom, autonomy, and a connection with nature are essential for human happiness. The trend towards big, bigger, biggest, and even mammoth-sized cities, is a by-product of gigantism but is at odds with any system that can make people happier. Decentralization and a more prominent role for small countries and cities can counterbalance rampant gigantism. This chapter shows that big cities must be human-sized if they are to remain livable. Gigacities do not make people happier. Clear criteria must therefore be established to avoid further derailments.

Derailing Demographics Crushes the Individual at the Expense of the Masses

Until the beginning of the nineteenth century the world population was relatively stable, and the earth supported roughly one billion inhabitants. This was followed by slow but steady growth until the dawn of the twentieth century. After the Second World War the earth's population rocketed, multiplying by about 2 per cent per year until the early 1980s. Annual growth may have tapered off to 1 per cent, but by then the total world population had swelled to five billion. Today our planet sustains almost eight billion people. While growth in the West is somewhat stagnant and even negative in some cases, a new population explosion is taking place on the world's largest continent: Africa. According to United Nations estimates, the population of the African continent will increase from just over one billion at the beginning of the twenty-first century to 4.5 billion by the year 2100. After that, Africa will even overtake Asia in terms of numbers. For the world this means a leap from 7.9 billion inhabitants to probably more than 11 billion. In two hundred years or so, the world's population will have increased sevenfold; if we go back to the beginning of the Industrial Revolution, we can even speak of a tenfold increase.

It is not only Africa's growth that poses a challenge; people are living much longer. The Swedish doctor and professor Hans Rosling rightly states that the world population is already on the rise today because adults are simply living longer.[25] Medical science will continue to improve, which will only lengthen life expectancy.

THE WOLVES OF YELLOWSTONE

This book is about balance, and here nature can always teach us valuable lessons. For this and other reasons I love the natural world, especially wild nature, large nature parks, mountains, and desolate areas. Nature always manages to find a new balance; she takes her time, and this has profound consequences that only gradually become clear. You are more likely to find me spending my holidays in a wilderness spot than on an overcrowded beach. (The latter is a good illustration of the pervasive gigantism and industrialization of our holidays.)

Yellowstone National Park in the United States is a fantastic natural park. One can go there for the tourist highlights, but the park also offers vast, lesser-known tracts of unspoiled nature. If you go just five hundred metres away from the attractions, you probably will not meet a single other tourist.

In 1907, faced with political pressure, the park's managers developed an eradication program designed to protect cattle in Yellowstone from predators. Hunters were given the green light to shoot as many wolves as they liked, and, less than twenty years later, the Yellowstone wolves had been expunged. As a result, the park's elk population skyrocketed, leading to overgrazing at the expense of several tree and plant species. For the same reason, Yellowstone also suffered from riverbed erosion and its associated disadvantages.

On YouTube is a video, viewed tens of millions of times, about a scheme to reintroduce wolves to Yellowstone. This was in 1995. Although only thirty-one wolves have been released, this has had a huge effect on the park.[26]

The wolves hunted the elk, which until then had had few natural enemies. The number of elk fell spectacularly as a result (see figure 5.6), and they were driven out of the riverbeds. Shrubs and trees, which would not have been able to take root because of the grazing herds, grew again. In turn, this new vegetation led to less erosion and caused the rivers in Yellowstone to meander more. In other words, a small number of wolves radically changed the Yellowstone landscape. Recent studies also revealed that the wolves thinned out the weaker members of the herd, stabilizing the elk population as a whole.[27]

Nature teaches us that small things can have enormous impact. The example of Yellowstone proves that one does not need to come up with big solutions to solve big problems. The solution to the issue of heavy erosion from a river that meandered too gently could have been a large dam, a massive structure on which engineers worked for years, and for which thousands of construction workers poured millions of tons of concrete that were delivered by thousands of trucks. Or the problem can be solved by the release of a handful of wolves into the wild.

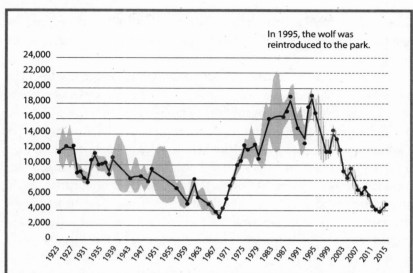

Figure 5.6   A few young wolves can make the difference: Number of elk in Yellowstone National Park, 1923–2016.

Source: Yellowstone Science, https://www.nps.gov/yell/learn/nature/wolf-restoration.htm.

Already, bigger ships, bigger ports, and bigger cities are being envisaged to feed and house these billions of new earthlings. Although there is copious scientific evidence that demographic growth leads to gigantism – which in turn fosters disease, crime, and inequality and makes people unhappy – no world leaders today dare to debate this problem. The spiralling rise in the world's population poses a direct threat not only to socio-economic life but also to our climate. The fact that this subject is not up for debate today has nothing to do with a dearth of facts or scientific insights but with a lack of political nerve and realistic thinking.

The same is true of gigantism: we must learn to think smaller and make our economy healthier again with minimal interventions that are closer to (human) nature. Nature also teaches us that dinosaurs were more vulnerable to climate change than smaller organisms such as insects and rodents were. The dinosaurs died out; the little ones survived. Today the biggest problem is the overpopulation of the earth by humans. We will solve this problem not by creating facilities to lift the world population from eleven billion to twenty billion but by making agreements to evolve from eleven billion earthlings to a smaller, more sustainable world population.

The impact of gigantism on society is obvious. Large entities offer advantages, such as economies of scale, but the social consequences are usually negative: stress, obesity, air pollution, cancer, burnout, and so on. This oversized scale is not human centred. The dehumanization of the economy has many faces. The Yellowstone metaphor should help us understand how an ecosystem can be affected by small changes – for instance, by a small band of wolves. It should come as no surprise that in an economic ecosystem a Walmart, an Ikea, a block of apartments, or – the opposite – a large park or a few playgrounds can have a significant impact on society. We underestimate the negative impact on our society of major economic decisions that are sustained over a long period of time. In addition, we ignore the importance of the small scale in our living environment.

So who are the "wolves of gigantism"? For me, they are the extra-ordinary teachers who instill character and faith in their pupils' own abilities and talents; the small shopkeeper who makes a difference each and every day; the entrepreneur who obstinately refuses to sell his or her business for big money; the politician or judge who refuses to give in to a powerful lobby or to corruption; the artist who inspires people with brand new and audacious art; and all the parents who admire their children when they colour outside the lines, and when they fall hard, comfort them and help them get back on their feet. You and I must be the ones to bare our teeth and be the wolves snapping at the heels of gigantism.

With this book I hope to change minds and convince policy-makers to consider small things that can have big consequences. The wolves in Yellowstone are a metaphor for the power of faith in the small things that can bring an ecosystem back into balance in a matter of decades.

FROM GROWTH OBSESSION
TO SUSTAINABLE GROWTH

The word *economy* is derived from the ancient Greek words *oikos* (house or family) and *nomos* (rule). It is about the rules of the house or one's community. Hence, economics is about the way in which people interact with each other, the rules of play, and the agreements that, round after round, determine the evolution of the results and shape one's "econosystem." Today it appears that the rules of play stimulate, or even overstimulate, "being big." This has implications beyond the purely economic. They affect all aspects of people and society. Besides the positive effects (cheap consumer goods, efficiency, and standardization, for example) there are also many negatives, as described in the previous chapter. The adverse effects of gigantism are enormous, and this will only become more evident in the future for more and more actors in the economic game.

Frustration is increasingly leading to the repudiation of the entire economic system with which we are familiar today: no more trade, no more international cooperation, no more companies, no more capitalism, no more growth, no more economics … The antiglobalization that we have witnessed since 1999 has evolved. Then there were protests against the World Trade Organization and free trade agreements, culminating in riots, known these days as the Battle of Seattle. It gave me pause for thought. More recently, 2018 witnessed the movement of *les gilets jaunes* (yellow vests): disaffected middle-class people who mobilized through social media and suddenly popped up in every city in France. The same frustration is evident in the climate movement and in the school protests first organized by Sweden's Greta Thunberg. Since the end of 2018 this movement has mushroomed, and Thunberg has been invited to speak to all kinds of organizations and heads of state.

Each time, one feels the protesters' anger at our economic model and at "capitalism." But Western capitalism does not have a monopoly on the excesses they all decry; these excesses are also inherent in communist regimes. Protesters are, however, correct in claiming than an equitable capitalist model should be able to fend off these excesses or deal with them efficiently and equitably. In my view, this is not happening, or not to a sufficient extent, due to a lack of capitalism and a surfeit of fake capitalism. Adam Smith's archetypal capitalism would not have sanctioned these excesses; today's gigantism is, then, a breeding ground for all these abuses and the subsequent dissent. In reality, economics is about people collaborating, creating things together, doing business, solving problems, and continually seeking better solutions. Economics is about people, not about a dehumanized yet efficient system.

Human beings are never satisfied with their current situation; they are curious about new experiences, new things. That is known as progress. There is indeed a risk of exaggerating in the other direction and bringing progress to a halt. An example of this is the movement to reject economic growth and pursue stagnation or even worse. This movement, also called degrowth, is now in full swing. But degrowth is equivalent to "no progress," which essentially amounts to restraining the human spirit. And if you really want to make people unhappy and frustrated, that is the perfect remedy.

Growth Is a Normal Human Ambition

For most non-economists, economic growth is an abstract concept because growth is something one cannot really feel. To most people in the Western world, the perceived temperature of between 0.5 and 1.5 per cent economic growth is virtually unnoticeable. Unless there is an economic boom or a severe recession, most people have no idea of a country's economic health. Average growth is too slow to be noticed every year. But with a ten-year period as a yardstick, one is more likely to notice that progress has been made. Most people identify this as "growth of comfort." They used to have a television set, a car, and a refrigerator; nowadays they show off their air-conditioning system, smart phones, and electronic games they have bought for their kids – and, of course, a Netflix subscription.

Over the past two centuries the Western economy grew an average of 2 per cent per year. Development was not always constant, however; there were periods of accelerated growth (such as in the boom time of the 1960s) and of sluggish growth (evident at the beginning of the nineteenth century). A growth of 2 per cent seems insignificant, but it does mean that the average level of prosperity doubles every thirty-five years. Every new generation starts in a completely new economic world. This immediately paints a different picture and shows how palpable and meaningful the long-term effect of growth is.

Before the Industrial Revolution, economic growth was almost non-existent. In some eras it was even negative. For example, the Western economy stagnated between the years 0 and 1000 CE, largely due to the collapse of the Roman Empire, which plunged Europe into the Dark Ages. From the year 1500 onwards a clear progression was evident, but growth levels did not exceed 0.5 per cent per year. The Netherlands rode the wave of economic growth, but there the economy expanded by roughly 0.5 per cent per year. In today's terms we would call that an almost stagnant economy. Perhaps we underestimate the growth in that epoch; after all, it was a time of significant technological advances. We can even refer to it as the first globalization boom: trade with Asia, Africa, and Latin America flourished, and shipbuilding, navigation, and finance underwent an astounding revolution.

Nevertheless, growth was limited. Economists still argue about the real causes. Some, such as the British demographer and economist Thomas Malthus (1766–1834), developed a pessimistic vision and preached that man would always run up against his limitations, especially in terms of raw materials and food. Productivity gains were also meagre because the main sources of energy were still man and animal. It was only with the advent of machinery, and in particular with the emergence of oil as the main energy source, that humankind achieved colossal productivity gains and thus enormous economic growth. After 1820, growth accelerated remarkably, in what we have come to call the Industrial Revolution, although it would be better to refer to this era as the "Capitalist Period."

Today the West is growing at a slower pace than the East. China is setting growth rates that are almost double those of the West each year, although even the Chinese growth rates have almost halved in comparison to those of ten years ago and are slowing further. Since 1973, China's average annual growth rate has been as high as 7.5 per cent, which equates to a doubling of Chinese wealth each decade. That rate has now declined, but Chinese growth today is the largest contributor to the expansion of the world economy. India and other Asian countries also have mesmerizing growth rates.

Aiming for zero growth is nonsensical for several reasons and is therefore not the solution to gigantism or other excesses of the economy. This is because economic growth is a corollary of various processes that are impossible to stop. Growth can have a variety of sources. We will consider some of them in the following paragraphs.

High Demographic Growth, or Growth by Stork

Countries with significant demographic growth naturally also enjoy robust economic growth. As the expanding population is drawn into economic life, the gross domestic product (GDP) – all that a country generates in income – will expand more rapidly. For this reason, to compare the economic performance of countries, economists usually calculate growth in GDP per capita. This allows them to objectify differences in population growth. Immigration is also a source of population growth. It has been an important factor in the United States, for instance, but also increasingly in Western Europe. The difference in growth between the United States and Europe can be explained almost entirely by the difference in demographic rates. The annual growth rate per capita (i.e., adjusted for demographic growth) in the European Union was 1.4 per cent from 1998 to 2018, as shown by figures from the World Bank.[1] The United States grew by 1.3 per cent annually over the same period. The rest of the growth is partly a result of accounting ploys because in the economic world, too, performance is presented in the most favorable light possible.

Convergence: Follow the Leader

It is a strategy with which racing cyclists are all too familiar: it is easier to ride in the slipstream of the cyclist in front than to generate the speed oneself. In the economy the same holds true: countries that experience rapid growth are often swept along by other countries with higher levels of prosperity. For a long time the economies of Eastern Europe grew, pulled along by their richer Western European counterparts. Europe used to benefit from the suction effect of the United States. China was elevated by the level of the West when Beijing opened up to the rest of the world. This also means that at a certain point the leader is confronted with an inhibiting head start: other countries copy the leader but with a better, higher-performing version.

Better Technology: Growth through Leadership

A country with a more superior or efficient technology or knowledge base will record higher economic growth over time; however, the disparities will be less dramatic as other countries progressively adopt the same technology. Robust growth is not necessarily an indication of a strong economy; it could equally be the result of high population growth. High growth per capita may indicate a suction or convergence effect. But if we look at the sources of growth, zero growth is not a feasible option for the world. There are no global or regional agreements on demographics. Borders and trade are open, so convergence is a given. And there are no bans on technological progress. Even if Europe collectively decided not to expand, it would not be able to impose this on the rest of the world. Moreover, the decision would quickly impoverish Europe, and Europeans would greatly miss out on technological leaps in the world at large.

The proponents of zero growth are thus wholly ignorant of the sources of economic growth. Growth does not necessarily mean "more"; growth can also mean "better." Enforcing zero growth would imply that one would no longer look for solutions to produce energy with less carbon dioxide. It would mean that we would cease to look for ways to eliminate the plastic soup in our rivers, seas, and oceans, that we would no longer conduct research into new cancer medications – after which the advocates of zero growth usually gaze at us in disbelief. Zero growth would also mean forbidding people to be creative, robbing the new generation of the urge to make the world a better place.

This does not mean that we need to aim for the maximum possible growth. In my view, more than 2 per cent growth per capita for a developed economy over a long period is achievable only with growth hormones, and that, as we know, leads to excesses. As a simple rule of thumb, you could say that the normal growth rate of a developed economy is between 0.5 per cent and 1.5 per cent a year, plus or minus its demographic growth. So when I argue for a slower economy, I am not talking about a stagnating economy at all. Here too, nature is a source of inspiration: trees that grow fast are less resilient; trees that grow slowly survive longer and are better able to withstand storms or crises. Rapid economic growth not only creates economic excesses, such as debt or bubbles, but can also destabilize societies and, as we also know, exhaust resources and produce undue levels of emissions. Slow economic growth offers a chance for humans to better adapt.

What Then Is the Problem with Economic Growth?

There are adverse effects associated with the current economic growth, which is based on higher energy consumption and causes high levels of pollution. There is a scientifically proven and direct link between CO_2 emissions and climate problems. At the same time, there is a link between the CO_2 in the atmosphere and the current economic model, which is driven by colossal energy consumption, based on fossil fuels. These detrimental effects, however, have to do less with the principle of economic growth than with the type of economic system we have. More than that, future economic expansion will, to a large extent, result from the solutions we are searching for to reverse the adverse effects of the economic system of the past.

Seeing economic growth as a problem and not as a solution is the most common mistake made by non-economists, activists, and myopic opinion makers. Pleading for sustainable growth is another story, and one with which I fully sympathize. But sustainable growth is hard to enforce; it is more likely to be triggered by economic incentives, such as rising prices. It also helps to understand the factors that cause unsustainable growth, some of which are the same factors that trigger gigantism. On the one hand, if we have a greater understanding of what sustainable growth is – and can stimulate it – then gigantism will be reined in. On the other hand, if we can do away with the incentives that cause gigantism, we will be one step closer to sustainable growth.

Not only is current economic growth too polluting, but its benefits are not equally distributed among the different generations. The current generation attempts to maximize economic growth with no thought for the consequences. Pollution is one such example. But the same is true – and I have already mentioned this several times – of debt growth. In the end, debts are a way to buy something today that one would only be able to buy in a few years' time. In other words, debts front-load economic growth. When it comes to investments – think of houses, schools, ICT, or infrastructure – you could argue that this is beneficial. However, in some cases even that is incorrect: once overcapacity is created, too much investment will only worsen the situation. Take cars or consumer goods, for example: if overcapacity occurs and the government encourages even more investment by making consumption cheaper, by making credit cheaper – lowering interest rates is a powerful tool – the problem is compounded. Governments suffering from growth difficulties wish to take so-called Keynesian measures and, with debt, embark on all kinds of futile major infrastructural schemes. Not only are these not economically fruitful, but they also constitute an attack on nature or people. Keynesian white elephants spur even greater gigantism.[2]

Public debts are one of the main reasons that states promote excessive economic growth, despite all its negative effects. Indeed, most countries and states are heavily indebted, not only in the form of visible debts (public debt) but also in the form of less visible debts – promises made but not matched by reserves. It is very enticing for politicians to make promises; they come in useful during an election. They can also be used to postpone problems to a later date because you will not actually solve them by going into debt or failing to set aside reserves. Most countries have not built up sufficient reserves for pensions and mounting health costs or for the environment and climate change.

Today governments have a vested interest in maintaining the highest possible growth rate because otherwise certain systems will implode. They would do well to realize that such a debt-driven policy causes excesses: excesses such as gigantism, but also overcapacity (which in turn leads to deflation) or detrimental social effects (for example, too many jobs with no real content, or the stifling of innovation, new jobs, and businesses). In this, the central banks are the governments' allies.

Keeping the old financial system afloat has become a very important objective, blinding governments to the long-term consequences of such interventions in the real economy and society.

The financial system is important, of course, but it is also self-stabilizing in the long run. If a financial system needs to be stabilized continually, either there is a structural problem or the governments are not satisfied with the signals that the financial system is sending them. If a currency is under strain, for example, the government may try to bolster that currency with bailout purchases. However, long-term interventions of this type have never been successful. Yet, if the financial markets believe that a government is taking measures to solve the problems, the pressure on the currency disappears straightaway.

When the financial system is under pressure due to temporary panic, interventions can indeed make sense. But the current sustained support for exchange rates, interest rates, and share prices all point to more profound economic problems. The financial system is a barometer of the economy. It can signal approaching storms and force policy-makers to take measures that they would not otherwise be able or dare to take. However, if you manipulate that barometer for a long time, you have no idea what the climate is actually like. You create an artificial economic greenhouse in which the residents believe that all is well, in which they believe that there are no climate problems. Such a policy is by no means sustainable. The real economy will not crash because the financial system is under pressure for a bit – quite the reverse. Recessions are commonplace. The long-term suppression of recessions and economic adjustments is unnatural and has strongly contributed to the current excesses.

Governments go to great lengths to inflate growth. As explained earlier, demographic growth is part and parcel of economic growth. That demographic growth, however, is completely neutral to the true underlying growth, which is driven by technological progress. But it is tempting for governments to capitalize on this factor: some countries still consider fertility important and thus try to maintain natural growth. Japan, whose population is shrinking, is then seen as an example to be avoided. But in reality Japan is not really saddled with an economic growth problem. Its per capita growth is in line with that of Europe and is hardly any lower than that of the United States. Japan is a country with a productive workforce, good institutions, top technology, and competitive businesses. It does, however, have a huge debt problem and an equally large pension problem, which is very problematic if one has a dwindling population.

In other words, a great deal of economic policy is aimed at objectives other than the real economy. Just think of pensions, debts, or exchange rates, to name but a few. This has far-reaching consequences for other areas of society, which I have already addressed. The blind pursuit of economic growth "whatever it takes" will be one of the main causes of future economic crises.

Zero growth, some suggest, may be a solution to economic derailments, but as I have already argued, such zero growth will only exacerbate the issues. What is more, this line of thinking is contrary to the drive of human beings to constantly improve and, in so doing, to invent new technologies, for example. I also believe that the current economic policy is not sustainable. The governments and central banks are themselves responsible for derailing the economic model a little more each year. The middle ground, sustainable growth, has become a catch-all term, which is why I would like to take the time to demystify it here.

Sustainable Growth

For a long time economists had a narrow view of their discipline. Economics had no need to consider very many elements; GDP and its optimization were the main objectives. Even today, generations of economists are being educated in highly theoretical economic worlds in which countries trade with each other and seek comparative advantages, while ignoring all the other impacts of that trade on the social and environmental spheres. Those same economists resent being criticized for their simplification of the real world and hide behind pseudo-mathematical equations to make it look as if economics were an exact science. Clearly it is not.

According to economic doctrine, free trade is beneficial always and everywhere. Any form of trade barrier must be shunned on pain of economic decline. This is not true. This economic dogmatism has led to unfettered international trade, which ultimately also aroused resistance, as in Seattle. I have sympathy for the protests against the Comprehensive Economic and Trade Agreement (CETA), which transforms the European Union and Canada into a transatlantic trade zone. Small regions such as Wallonia, in particular, were vehemently opposed to that trade agreement. I will not claim that renouncing international trade is any better, but the associated social and, for example, environmental aspects can no longer be ignored. Trade with China may be ideal from a strictly economic perspective, but such trade also entails grave social consequences. Some aspects are very beneficial for China (more jobs, a reduction in poverty), but there are also many unfavorable consequences (exploitation of children, non-compliance with health and safety standards, and massive pollution). We are seeing something similar at the other end of the trade spectrum: cheap consumer goods, and the disappearance of a number of skills and activities.

Universities still too often train traditional economists, who "optimize" the economy in theoretical frameworks. The simulations of supply or demand shocks are hammered home, with all the potential effects on government spending, investment, and consumption, but rarely are economists encouraged to look beyond their field of expertise. How does it affect people, society, happiness or health, climate, and the environment?

The British economist Richard Layard, whose book *Happiness* (2011) sought new economic and managerial strategies to increase happiness in society, broke new ground. Many others followed in his footsteps. In his book *Capital in the Twenty-First Century* the Frenchman Thomas Piketty demonstrated the impact of capital on inequality and, in doing so, sent a wake-up call to politicians. Although Piketty's work, in my opinion, contains fundamental errors – the time series on capital, for example, has a significant bias to winners,[3] which means that capital losses due to wars, bankruptcies, and other expropriations are underestimated[4] – he has greatly broadened the scope of economists. Kate Raworth, an economist at Oxford University's Climate Change Department, wrote the book *Donut Economics* in 2017, in which she closely links the economy to the limitations of the earth and the climate.

Many of these thinkers are deemed "left-wing" by traditional economists – an adjective that is actually irrelevant. After all, it is not at all leftist to not take a narrow view of the economic domain but broaden it to include society, the environment, and the place of man. Economics, climate science, and philosophy thus merge into new insights that make the economy more balanced. That is not left-wing, but simply very healthy.

Sustainability has to do with balance, with a long-term vision and with the aim of not harming others and nature. That is why the concept is so simple to summarize:

- *Sustainable growth is neutral across generations*: there are no new debts, except for productive investments; no pollution that needs to be cleaned up later; no damage to people or the earth.

- *Sustainable growth does not lead to social distortions*: it protects humanity and society and does not disadvantage a social class or privilege a particular category.

It is difficult to compare economic growth between countries and regions. Sustainable growth can easily slow down for years, but it can be accompanied by the strengthening of social cohesion, improvement of the ecological footprint, or even the reduction of debts. Germany, Switzerland, the Scandinavian countries, and the Netherlands are not growth champions, but they all score very highly in terms of sustainability.

There is also a simpler definition: growth that leads to gigantism is not sustainable growth. More to the point, we will have an increasingly competitive economy with giants on one side and a growing group of zombie corporations on the other. They are two sides of the same economic coin.

Giants and Zombies

In the preceding chapters I outlined a host of the deleterious effects of gigantism. Most were of a socio-economic nature. For some time now, economists have been puzzling over why productivity growth in the economy has been so low, even negative in many countries, over the past decade, while technological progress has been accelerating. Productivity growth was particularly strong in the 1990s but began slowing when the technology bubble peaked just after the millennium transition. Since then it has been on a downward trend.

This lull is obviously counterintuitive: one would expect the technology boom to accelerate productivity growth. In fact, the statistics are so counterintuitive that some economists have begun to doubt their accuracy – unjustifiably so because it is not the measurement of GDP that is the problem. Indeed, many changes are already being made to the calculation of GDP to include those qualitative (technological) improvements: 20 per cent of US GDP is determined by so-called hedonistic (quality) adjustments. Some might call those adjustments "air" because they are not tangible. They are quality improvements that are not reflected in price: your computer is faster, your phone smarter, and your car safer (and smarter). The price of all these devices has remained stable or sometimes even dropped. So it is only natural to factor them into GDP calculations. Most OECD countries use these hedonistic adjustments, just as immaterial (intangible) assets often contribute substantially to the GDP.

If the drop in productivity is not a measurement problem, is it perhaps a timing problem? This is the thesis of Erik Brynjolfsson and Andrew McAfee, two researchers at the prestigious Massachusetts Institute of Technology and the authors of *Race against the Machine*. The duo assumes that everything is yet to come. Economists, however, rarely agree. The well-known American economist Robert Gordon is pessimistic. He argues that innovation is really not all that spectacular; it has delivered an overabundance of devices and too little impetus to productivity growth. In any case, Gordon argues, it cannot compensate for the negative impact of demographics (aging).[5]

Macroeconomists do not agree on the reasons for this situation, perhaps because their approach is too macro, whereas the answer is more likely to be found at the micro-level of firms. A recent OECD study shows that productivity gains are only being made by a small number of frontier firms, and all other companies stopped making productivity gains in 2000 (see figure 6.1).[6] The giants are the ones that reap all the productivity rewards, while negatively affecting the economy as a whole. Well-known digital global players (such as Google, Apple, and Amazon) and more traditional giants (such as the major car makers, the cosmetics group L'Oréal, or the food group Nestlé) have recorded impressive productivity gains since 2000. They create more and more income per employee. But the other companies stagnated in terms of productivity. How can this discrepancy be explained?

OECD specialists are looking to innovation for the answer, but there are two other key phenomena that may offer a more adequate explanation. Firstly, statistics show that within the OECD there is a growing group of non-viable companies. These are companies that pile up losses year upon year but nevertheless survive for a long time – thanks to the policy of ultra-low interest rates, easy credit, and all manner of subsidies and other government aid. Secondly, the big corporations can finance themselves considerably more cheaply than the small ones can, on both the equity and the debt markets. The central bank amplifies this effect with the buy-back programs mentioned earlier, which are available to large companies but not to small ones.

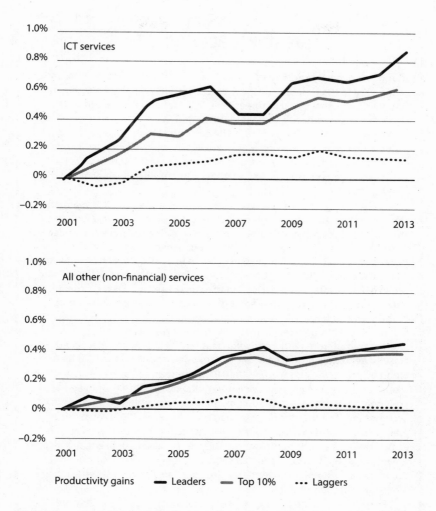

Figure 6.1   The winner takes all: A small number of firms accounts for almost all productivity gains

Source: Andrews, Criscuolo, and Gal, *The Best versus the Rest*, based on the Orbis database.

Zombie companies and giants are therefore the result of both the monetary policy since 2000 and other economic stimuli, an unintentional but nevertheless economic evolution that is now emerging in the statistics. In order to restore productivity, the financial sector should be stimulated to stop keeping zombie companies alive artificially. Zombie companies prefer not to be named. After all, they would then blame

THE GLOBAL PONZI SCHEME

Carlo Ponzi, better known as Charles Ponzi,[7] was born in Italy in 1882 and emigrated to the United States, where he combined small jobs with petty crime. He was sentenced to three years' imprisonment in Canada and later to two years' imprisonment in the United States. From 1920 onwards, however, he saw the bigger picture: he exploited his charm and acting talent and became a professional swindler. His scam, which is still known today as the Ponzi scheme, consists of luring investors (speculators) with very high potential returns and paying them with the deposits of new customers.[8]

Since the high returns are not achieved (if they are invested at all), the leader of the fraudulent scheme must constantly motivate new investors to join and discourage would-be leavers from doing so. Ponzi succeeded only briefly; after just one year his notorious scheme imploded. The fraudster promised a profit of 50 per cent in forty-five days and as much as a 100 per cent in a hundred days. However, his actual return was zero, and even negative after costs. So he had to entice ever-more new customers to pay his huge returns. Once an outflow started, it became impossible to continue his scheme.

Subsequent fraudsters who followed in Ponzi's footsteps, such as Bernie Madoff, Tom Pettis, and Allen Stanford, realized that they could last longer if they promised lower returns. Madoff built a USD 65 billion fund by promising his investors only 10 per cent a year, but a very stable return. His clients were mainly charities, and he was legally obliged to pay out only 5 per cent a year. Madoff might have been able to continue his scheme for life if the stock market had not crashed in 2008, when prices fell by 38 per cent in a few months, even as he claimed to have achieved a positive return of almost 6 per cent. If you promise 10 per cent and in reality achieve 8 per cent and can still attract new customers, your Ponzi scheme can last until a major crisis. Crises are also good excuses for the implosion of such a bubble.

Ponzi schemes are the opposite of sustainable structures. They are inherently unstable and owe their success to the ignorance of those who join them and to the selling of empty promises. If we look at today's world economy through this lens, we will discover other huge Ponzi schemes.

Perhaps the world's biggest Ponzi scheme is social security in Europe. Here, ever-larger commitments are made, while the economic growth to pay all those benefits is lower with every decade. Meanwhile, the number of people entering (those paying for social security) is decreasing due to demographics, and those receiving the benefits are increasing. Pension schemes in Europe that are based not on the capitalization system (a system in which pensions are grounded in savings and investments, like pension funds in the Netherlands) but on the system of repartition (where the young pay for the pensions of the old, without accumulating funds) are by definition Ponzi schemes. As soon as demographics falter (and aging increases), a smaller number of young people must pay for the pensions of an ever-larger group of elderly. If the pledges to those older people then increase, the pension scheme is in danger of collapsing, just like Charles Ponzi's or Bernie Madoff's scheme.

Politicians are the Bernie Madoffs who pledge good returns and hope that the pension scheme will last their time without collapsing. Meanwhile, our climate management too is a Ponzi scheme: humans pump more and more greenhouse gases into the atmosphere, more than earth is able to absorb by natural means. If we look even further, we can see that global debts are expanding like a Ponzi scheme. Ever-higher debts have to be placed, while the appetite to buy them decreases. In order to sustain the debt "Ponzi" scheme, central banks would have to start buying up the debt themselves, which they did for a long time. And they have lowered interest rates, although this did not help to find new entrants.

What about bitcoin? A Ponzi scheme must meet three conditions: the valuation is intrinsically very low or impossible to determine; the inflows are manipulated by insiders, and all the necessary means are deployed to whet the appetite; and once the outflow starts, panic sets in and no buyers can be found. Bitcoin meets these three criteria beautifully. It is a perfected, digital Ponzi scheme, the first scheme with a truly global reach. Bitcoin may hold some tiny value, but it is digital hot air. As recent events show, Ponzi schemes unravel when confidence fades and liquidity problems arise.

A Ponzi scheme is an anti-establishment scheme. Charles Ponzi should have been posthumously awarded the Riksbank Nobel Prize, better known as the Nobel Prize in Economics, for his major contribution to today's economic and financial systems.[9]

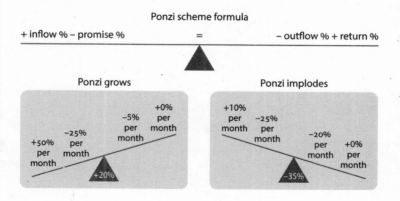

Figure 6.2   Ponzi scheme: The "success formula"

the author for their (long overdue) demise. Zombie companies can be recognized by their systematic-problem denial, their conservative business models, their regular restructuring and downsizing, and their high debt levels. But they also openly or covertly turn to the government for support. Owing to their close historical contacts with those authorities or with interest groups, they also manage to stave off competitors for a long time through complex rules or entry barriers. The elimination of such zombies (which sometimes span almost an entire sector) could oxygenate a large number of new, young companies that could make the economy more dynamic. This is what Europe needs, above all. Down with the zombies! Long live entrepreneurship! Higher interest rates, a tighter credit policy, and healthier banks would contribute to this, as would scrapping the lunatic monetary policies of the European Central Bank, the US Federal Reserve, the Bank of Japan, and other central banks. Perhaps we are now witnessing the first signs of a turn for the better, as central banks are tightening their decade-long lose policies.

Remember that there are giants on the one side and a myriad of zombie companies on the other. This again proves that the current economic system is not leading to a sustainable economic situation and that we do not have true capitalism today.

7

SMALLER, SLOWER, AND MORE HUMAN

The world economy is spinning further and further away from a sustainable equilibrium. Compare it to a game in which, during each new round, one of the players accumulates more and more points, while the others no longer enter the game – giants on one side, zombies on the other, and unhappy people in between. The incidence of diseases of affluence is increasing because that kind of economy pushes people further away from economic life. Unsustainable debt growth has to push economic growth higher than would be possible on its own. Meanwhile the economy spews out more greenhouse gases than the earth can absorb. With each new round in this crazy economic game, the excesses intensify. It is clear that patching up the economy or holding back will not turn the tide; a more profound readjustment is required. Raising problems and issues is one thing, but what about the solutions?

Some economists reject the entire system and become anticapitalists, antiglobalists, or anarchists. Others seek refuge in structures that have been shown to end in similarly huge excesses, albeit in other areas: communism or Marxism. The solution cannot be to drift from one extreme to the other. Many may find my criticism of gigantism and big business extreme, but I hope they will face the facts. There is overwhelming evidence that the economy provides too many incentives to grow to a size that puts the economy on an unsustainable path and dehumanizes it in the process.

Logically, I will therefore argue in favour of the smaller, or at least the "less big": an economy on a human scale, a socio-economic system that does not derail. For many, however, small has negative connotations: homely, for example, or too small-town, provincial, and tailored to the small fry of this world, too little ambition, underachieving, not customized to ingenious individuals, an impediment, and so on.

That is certainly not the economic model we should be moving towards. We should not reject the benefits of globalization and the progress made in recent decades. There is no need to shut down the Internet or ban multinational corporations. This is not an antiglobalization philosophy but an urgent plea to rethink our current derailed globalization and, above all, to return to the origins of capitalism, the humane and balanced capitalism of Adam Smith.

The powerful engine of a more balanced world economy and society is decentralization. Centralization, elevation to a higher level, was too often presented as the answer to every problem. The consequence has been ever-larger bureaucratic and hierarchical pyramids. These organizations thrive best when they become larger and larger. Companies, as well as countries or NGOs, have therefore – willingly or unwillingly – striven for ever-greater size. Locally, too, people are increasingly looking at centralization and scale as a solution to increase efficiency, and schools, hospitals, and libraries have become giants. In most cases this centralization has increased their efficiency in economic terms,[1] but in other respects it has diminished their efficiency. Not only are these gigantic organizations further away than ever from the people they are intended to serve, but also they may have excluded certain categories and thereby reduced social mobility. Scale may be one of the reasons that pupils or patients no longer feel drawn to certain schools or hospitals: they feel that their situation is not adequately taken into account, thereby worsening their mental well-being. In recent decades, centralized thinking has crept silently into our society, probably with the best of intentions.

Not only has centralized thinking led to a greater distance from people, but also it has created completely different functions: management functions are required, as well as control functions to verify that everyone is adhering to the agreed procedures and rules. As a result, the focus shifts more to the managing of these organizations instead of to the central purpose for which these institutions were established: educating young people, for example, or treating patients. The purely economic thinkers preached centralization because it brings economic efficiency, but they failed to include the other dimensions – social and environmental, for example – in their models or reflections. It is this one-dimensional thinking that is at the root of gigantism.

Decentralization brings organizations closer to the people, empowering those who create real value (to use a hip verb, decentralization "empowers" them), but it also strengthens social cohesion. Indeed, a library in a small town may not seem as efficient as a mega-library in a nearby big city, but that small local library also serves as a meeting place, a place where all generations of a community come together, often run by voluntaries. They know each other, or get to know each other, by sharing tips on books or what to read, or simply by sneaking a peek at what their neighbour is reading. In a city the giant library will be more efficient and cheaper but also more anonymous and less community-building. It will be run by professionals and managers. The same applies to schools. Large educational institutions are more economically efficient, but very often they miss the mark. A school should also educate each individual to the best of its ability, and it plays an important role in the local community. In the drive for efficiency we have lost sight of the individual and his or her community.

Thinking smaller does not mean sacrificing economic efficiency in the end. One of the great advocates of decentralization is the Lebanese-American scientist, former derivatives trader, and author Nassim Nicholas Taleb. In *The Black Swan* and *Antifragile*, he defends smaller entities: "On paper it seems much more efficient to be big – because then you can have economies of scale. But in reality, it is much more efficient to be small … But an elephant can break a leg very easily, whereas you can toss a mouse out of a window and it'll be fine. Size makes you fragile."[2] The fact that large systems are fragile and should therefore be better decentralized is also at the basis of the World Wide Web, the Internet. Forty years ago the government and the army relied heavily on large mainframes for their organization. However, these large, powerful computers to which several terminals can be connected were very vulnerable to targeted attacks. By the use of networks of decentralized and smaller computers, it was possible to make the system more resilient and flexible.

Decentralized systems not only make people less vulnerable to the failure of one large system but also promote diversity. If a central system is conceived incorrectly, there is a high risk that everything will cease to work.[3] Not so with decentralized systems: there you will still be able to use various other concepts. This diversity also has unexpected consequences and even leads to serendipity: some systems will surprise you because they turn out to be exceptionally good performers. The more one experiments, the greater will be the chance of discovering new things!

There is another important reason for further decentralization: central systems do not encourage competition, and that leads to impoverishment. The greater the number of decentralized organizations, the greater the choice, and the smaller the step to switch from a failing local organization to a nearby alternative. Imagine you have one large school in a twenty-kilometre (twelve-mile) radius, with 2,500 pupils. Or ten schools in the same region with 250 pupils. Both types of school are guaranteed to be organized completely differently: the big school will have various management layers, while the network of small schools will have much less or none at all; the large school will create new roles that, in the network of small schools, are simply carried out by teachers. For pupils, the network of small schools will also seem much less daunting than that one large school. Some specialization might also arise in the network, with a school for athletic, musical, technical, or tech-savvy students, and one for gifted children. This is not possible in the centralized school. An added and not unimportant disadvantage is that, if that school does not offer a high quality of education, the centrally organized system offers few alternatives. In the decentralized system, pupils and their parents still have nine options left.

The school management example clearly shows that decentralized systems can only be economically efficient if other scenarios are considered in addition to one-dimensional, poorly defined economic parameters. There is no question that dismantling centralized systems has many positive benefits, but the question arises, Why did we not decentralize more in recent decades? One thing is certain: for a long time, gigantism was able to count on a loyal group of fans. The alternatives only stood a chance when the dominant system began to flounder. Also, under pressure from the lobbyists, economists and policy-makers offered too little intellectual resistance for some time. This occurred even in so-called soft sectors, such as education or health care. The idea of decentralization is only emerging now because we have just begun to have the technology to make it possible. The recent COVID-19 crisis, by the way, demonstrated once again the strength of decentralization. Researchers found that countries that were more decentralized managed the crisis better than those that were more centralized.[4]

In this respect, the difference in approach between Germany and Italy is exemplary. Germany is a highly decentralized country and experienced far fewer legal and political tensions during the management of the pandemic than the less decentralized Italy did. This was due to the long-standing tradition of coordination and cooperation between the different decentralized units and a clear division of competences between the German states and the federal government. In a study the World Health Organization stated that centralization increased when the government was able to take widely supported decisions, and decentralization increased when more difficult and unpopular decisions were required.[5] It demonstrates that in times of crisis decentralization results in flexibility and agility, and centralization in standardization and rigidity.

Triggers of Decentralization and Size Reduction

There are five reasons we will see more decentralization in the coming decades. Call them the seeds of the "gigantism revolution." Today the trend towards "ever larger" is already past its peak, as the discontinuation of the A380 airliner and the grounding of the *Ever Given* in the Suez Canal illustrate. It can only be sufficiently mitigated if government and politics also do their bit. If not, gigantism will continue to wreak havoc in the future. Each of the five triggers is a factor that swings the pendulum in the other direction. They are forces that provide advantages to "downsizing" and decentralized systems. They include technology, human preference, the failure of "bigness," robustness and loyalty. We could call them the five trump cards for downsizing.

Technology as an Enabler of Smaller Organizations

In the past, large bureaucratic organizations tended.to settle in one central place because that was the only way for the various echelons of the organization to communicate with each other quickly and efficiently. Consider the Roman Catholic Church in the past. Or an emperor or a king. Great armies have a central command; the Pentagon is one example. Large companies and government agencies also have a predilection for this centralized approach. The first large computers amplified this centralization because they were very costly and very cumbersome; they filled an entire building, and only very large organizations could afford them.

It was the invention of the personal computer that provided the first impetus for more decentralization. The Internet, and later the smart phone, greatly accelerated that process. Zoom, Skype, Teams, and other conferencing tools are constantly improving and form the basis of decentralized organizations that combine efficiency (less travel) with robustness (no mainframe, fewer total system failures). Another advantage is that they do not need to be operated continuously. Small organizations today have much more computing, information, and communication power than the old, large organizations of the past did. Technology has given an enormous boost to creative individuals, entrepreneurship, flexible organizations, and local entrepreneurship. Large, unwieldy, centralized bureaucracies are no longer a match for the agile, high-performing small organizations. So it is ironic that the big tech giants are providing the weapons to fight gigantism!

Human Preference

People choose things that give them pleasure or enjoyment or that offer comfort and security. Large is impersonal, cold, and distant. Small is seen as warmer and more accessible. If one is about to get married and can choose between a large, chilly church and a small, cozy chapel, the decision will not take long, unless one is the king or would like to be one. People prefer personal services tailored to their individuality – which, in large organizations, is hard to achieve.

Centralization will always need to offer something extra to compensate for the lack of personal service: more goods and services, for example, or cheaper products, thanks to efficiency.

Could it be that decentralization is closer to ordinary people, while centralization is more for the elite? Doesn't a highly centralized organization tend to focus on the ego, while a decentralized organization focuses on the person, the individual, the co-worker?

The Failure of "Big"

Big seems to be bumping up against its limits. In the financial sector the large banks have barely survived a couple of heart attacks. Central banks are having to intervene with greater regularity and have become like giant "bad banks," carrying debt paper that the banks have sold to them. In the past they intervened infrequently, then gradually more often, then every few months, and today central banks have necessarily become day traders to keep the system ostensibly stable. The end of the A380, the blocking of the Suez Canal by the *Ever Given*, and a growing number of ghost shopping malls indicate that something might be changing.

Decentralization has already started in certain sectors. The Internet has done so in technology. The energy sector is gradually shifting from large centralized production to smartly linked, decentralized systems, a global energy web. In the political arena, too, "big" is no longer the sole solution. The European Union appears to be reaching the limits of enlargement and, thanks to Brexit, has taken a step in the other direction for the first time. Russia, too, has disintegrated into several smaller parts. And the question is whether China and the United States can each remain one big bloc. Even in the United States, regions such as California are less and less attracted to Washington and the central power of the president; there are also calls for more autonomy. China appears to be a massive and monolithic bloc, ruled with "enlightened" despotism by the Communist Party. However, appearances can be deceptive: even the Communist Party must employ sophisticated technology – facial recognition, for example – in order to monitor its residents and award them points. Chinese who score badly become pariahs. Various population groups are mobilizing (not only in Tibet), and the hard hand of the Chinese leadership remains hidden from Western cameras and social media. Sooner or later, it will be clear that a liberal capitalist model and a centrally led communist model are an impossible match.

At some point, big will reach its limits, and when expansion is out of the question, downsizing will suddenly become a new dynamic that can rapidly gain momentum. The Soviet Union and the former Yugoslavia taught us this. The same trend is apparent in companies as well. An example is the recent troubles at General Electric. This American conglomerate, active in technology, electronics, and services, was for many years a giant with so-called superhuman CEOs such as Jack Welch and Jeffrey Immelt, who both recorded their success formulas in management bestsellers. But apparently their recipe for success was not particularly sustainable. Today the once so powerful General Electric has withered away, is burdened by enormous debts, and has a lack of forward-looking activity and, above all, a total lack of agility. IBM is hard pressed to be innovative and is increasingly becoming a ministry

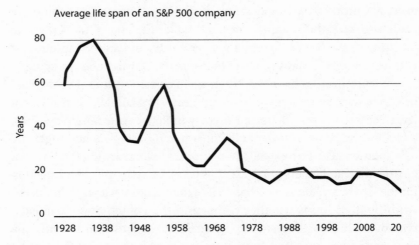

Figure 7.1   Large companies are vulnerable: Declining life expectancy of
large companies

Sources: s&p; Deloitte; The Shift Index.

of informatics. Innovation in large companies is tough; it is thwarted
because it might threaten existing business and especially existing
positions of power.

It seems a paradox: companies are becoming larger, but at the same
time the average lifespan of companies has decreased in recent decades
(see figure 7.1). In.the past the very biggest corporations (e.g., those in
the s&p 500 stock market index) easily attained an age of more than
sixty years. Today we see that the lifespan has declined significantly
and is now just under ten years on average. So disruption also makes
large companies fragile. The giants are increasingly in danger of being
ousted by the fast-growing, up-and-coming new giants. The survival
of the fittest rages on, although the top ten spots seem far more solidly
entrenched than the next 490 places.

Not only companies but also other large organizations run the risk of
reaching their limits and thus becoming vulnerable. The great fear of the
European Union is that Brexit might trigger further disintegration. In a
large group there is always discord. That the negotiations dragged on for
so long had as much to do with Britain's shaky political leadership as it

did with Europe's fear that a fast and too sweet deal would make other member states think twice. So far, the impact of Brexit has been less than positive for Britain, although the COVID-19 crisis naturally complicates the analysis. But it is not guaranteed to damage the economy for long. We should never underestimate the resilience of a small nation fighting for its prosperity, especially when it has major assets at its disposal and can also hand out fiscal favours.

Separation does indeed cause suffering, but sometimes that is the price that a nation, a part of an organization, or simply a number of people are prepared to pay to attain greater individuality, autonomy, or proximity, all of which they no longer find in large, centrally run organizations.

Voices calling for less Europe or a different Europe cannot simply be dismissed as populist. Just as Trumpism can largely be explained by big capitalism in the United States, the rapid expansion and the urge to become as big as the United States are also causes of resistance in Europe. It would thus be wise to address the causes rather than simply focus on the consequences.

I predict that the trend towards the smaller, and greater autonomy, will not stop. A region such as Catalonia will be imitated in its pursuit of increased autonomy, countries from the European Union will want to leave the euro, and large states will break up into more loosely connected, decentralized states. This does not need to be a negative development, and it does not have to spell the end of the European Union, NATO, the World Trade Organization, the euro, or any other institution. In time, we will see the same trend in the corporate giants, driven by innovation, entrepreneurship, or simply because the regulator obliges them to do so.

Robustness

The Internet is a decentralized system by definition. It was developed by the US military, among others, to make its technical infrastructure more robust. If one computer failed, there were other centres that could take over; a network was needed to regulate the bypass, and the Internet was born.

The same robustness and performance can be found in a number of countries. Switzerland always leads the list of the most competitive countries and also scores highly in terms of sustainability, public confidence, and stability. Switzerland owes this, among other things, to its policy, which has a low degree of centralization, and to its organization, in which powers are highly decentralized. The cantons and municipalities have many powers that would be managed centrally in other countries. The advantage is that the Swiss people are closely involved in these policies and never have the feeling that politics does not concern them. Moreover, the Swiss also take care of their public goods, ranging from park benches to public air-raid shelters. In fact, Switzerland today has the system that the founding fathers of the United States had in mind in the eighteenth century: a small government and a great deal of private initiative. Switzerland could have been invented by Adam Smith, but had already been in existence for a few centuries before his time. The challenge is to maintain such a philosophy, as a result of what is known as Wagner's law:[6] as a country becomes more prosperous and the private sector creates more value, there is a tendency to redistribute that value, causing the government to expand. Indeed, one sees government expansion and centralization in all prosperous countries. Still, Switzerland kept its lean structure as wealth grew and continues to grow steadily; its GDP per capita is much higher than that of the Eurozone and any individual country.

Decentralized systems are more robust than centralized systems due to a combination of two factors: the transmission of central preferences, and local flexibility. An example of such a central preference is the constitution of a country – or the DNA of a company. Local flexibility is important in order to be able to accentuate or adapt to the necessary differences that may exist locally. If a server goes down on the Internet, it will not cause a problem, because others can take over the role of the defective unit without forgetting the protocols.

Large, centrally managed entities, however, are extremely vulnerable. This has been amply demonstrated in the past. The Roman Empire, the Soviet Union, the Catholic Church, and large companies recognized the problems too late because they were centrally organized. Losing touch with the base is a major challenge for large, centralized organizations. The recovery of such an organization is not made top-down, but bottom-up, by the employees, the parish, and by entrepreneurship in strong business units.

Nassim Nicholas Taleb is an advocate of decentralization because it is "antifragile" and a strong form of government. Decentralized societies and companies actually grow stronger as they come under more pressure. The pressure disperses throughout the entire network, so that the central system does not have to absorb everything. Taleb is not one to shy away from making bold statements. On Twitter in 2016, he fired off the following: "Decentralisation is a nightmare for lobbyists."[7] If you read *Antifragile*, you will understand his reasoning perfectly. Lobbyists always argue for centralization because it is easier for them to grasp. Decentralized systems are much harder to influence. For this reason they are so important for a democracy. Central systems end in dictatorship. Decentralized systems guarantee that people still have their say. Long live democracy! Long live the decentralized system!

Loyalty

Centralized systems are often based on a power structure. By contrast, the "glue" of decentralized systems is loyalty. Economists tend to focus too much on the measurable factors (such as gross domestic product, corporate profits, or wages) and underestimate the softer and less easily measured elements (such as trust, happiness, and loyalty). Maybe that is why economists tend to think in a centralist way, and philosophers in a more human way.

Loyalty is essential to hold an organization or country together. How loyal would the inhabitants of Hungary, Poland, and the former Czechoslovakia have been to the Soviet Union in the 1970s? Or later, those in Kazakhstan, Uzbekistan, and Ukraine? Enforcing military loyalty from Moscow is difficult in any of the most remote regions.

The same applies in large companies. How strong was loyalty within Fortis on the eve of its collapse? As the bank insurer had grown so quickly, the employees never considered themselves as part of Fortis, but still as part of the staff of Generale Bank, AG Insurance, ASLK, or NMKN (which was a government bank for a long time), AMEV (a Dutch insurer), VSB, ASR, or private bank MeesPierson. Staff members called themselves, for example, a Generale Bank employee or an ASLKer. Fortis was a management concept that was far removed from the shop floor. A similar phenomenon has occurred in many companies over the past twenty-five years: mergers create artificially coherent groups that look very diverse on the inside. Employees are less loyal to the acquirer than to the company for which they originally started working. The same goes for the customers. Even the shareholders have little loyalty to the company because of this kind of expansion. It is all about the money, not about a connection with employees or customers.

Companies with loyal customers are stronger than companies that lure customers with temporary promotional stunts. Likewise, in difficult times, loyal employees or loyal shareholders make the difference: sharing success is easy, but fighting for a company because you are a loyal employee can create far more value in the long run. Triple loyalty (shareholders, customers, and employees) is a rare phenomenon, but it forms a triple-component adhesive. That is why family businesses are so strong: they build on that family loyalty. Partnerships or cooperative structures do the same. Although some partnerships are huge (such as the large accounting firms), scalability is generally more difficult. After all, the personal touch is key.

What applies to companies also applies to countries and other organizations. How loyal will EU countries still be to the European Union when they no longer enjoy its benefits? How loyal are the European Union's employees to the values of the Union compared with the huge tax benefits they receive? And how attuned are EU citizens to what is happening in Brussels? If a large, expanding organization does not have triple loyalty (from employees, shareholders, customers), the "glue" vanishes and the centrally managed organization can easily fall apart, especially in the event of major setbacks such as a crisis. This was striking during the COVID-19 pandemic when employees spontaneously assumed responsibility and mobilized to deal with the crisis.

Decentralized organizations are less vulnerable to lack of loyalty because there is a high level of loyalty at the local level. Decentralized entities are loyal to other sub-entities due to their own self-interest, namely their freedom. If a crisis occurs in another decentralized entity, they consider themselves loyal allies. After all, they would expect the same if something were to happen to them. This loyalty is entirely unrelated to a central authority that must enforce loyalty.

A stronger central authority combined with more local friction leads to tensions. Decentralized forces are naturally present, while central counterforces must continue to convince people of their added value.

Gigantism Is Not Irreversible

The five decentralizing forces – technology, human preference, the failure of "bigness," robustness, and loyalty – render giants vulnerable. At such fragile moments, when giants suffer other derailments, the pendulum can swing quickly in the opposite direction. Giants can suffocate under their own weight. A huge debt burden, for example, is one such aggravating factor. Equally, lack of innovation can cause giants to fall fast and hard. It is simple for the central leadership in China to make decisions, for example, yet a decentralized organization in which each component is self-managing would be able to make decisions faster and more flexibly. As a result, it can solve problems before they become life-threatening.

There is a long list of multinationals that realized too late that change was necessary. Kodak had the technology of the digital camera sitting in its drawer for a very long time but wanted to milk its old, analogue technology for as long as possible. For years, Nokia, a Finnish multinational, had a big lead in the field of mobile telephony, partly because, in the 1990s, after having left the Soviet bloc, the Finns did not develop telephony with fixed lines but implemented a new technology straight away. In 2000, Nokia was one of the largest corporations worldwide, yet it completely failed to make the switch to smart phones. For a long time, it was convinced that Apple's iPhone would be nothing more than a niche product. But five years after the launch of the iPhone, Nokia had lost 92 per cent of its market value. The Canadian BlackBerry, originally called Research in Motion, not only stuck to its successful technology for too long but also underestimated the power of innovation and the changing needs of its users. The BlackBerry devices were smarter than the first mobile phones and were particularly appreciated by business people. However, the makers did not realize that the functionalities of a mobile phone would increase exponentially and that smart phones would no longer remain exclusive gadgets for business people but would appeal to all mobile phone users. The Apple iPhone arrived and killed off the BlackBerry overnight.

When they started out, these companies were innovative and small, with short lines of communication. As their success grew, the more complex and even chaotic they became. As a result, their agility waned and information reached central management too slowly or incompletely. That is one of the fundamental problems facing giants: change happens more rapidly from below than from above. A giant is weakened by bottom-up processes to which a top-down answer cannot be given swiftly or resolutely.

The beer giants, for example, are less vulnerable to each other (Heineken versus AB InBev) than to the threat of changing tastes or of the thousands of microbreweries that have sprung up. The combination of IPAs (India pale ales) – trendy specialty beers from often small, artisanal breweries that use more hops in the production process – and, for example, the legalization of marijuana is potentially a much greater threat to the giant brewers than a new beer from a competitor or a (temporary) price war. Only then will the weaknesses of the beer giants become visible: excessively high debt positions or, for example, the arrogance of a CEO. The latter constitutes a threat to many large companies because the culture of inviolability is an ideal breeding ground for alpha males and arrogance in general.

In 2008 we also saw an abundance of hubris in the banking sector. Today that same hubris is rearing its head again, as the memory of the financial crisis fades. As I said, the pity of failing giants is that they do not just fall over; because of their size they are often considered too big to fail. It would be healthier for the entire banking sector if reckless banks were to fall and make way for smaller, more sustainable banks.

Deglobalization

Brexit did not simply fall out of the sky. Organizations that become larger and more powerful run the risk of alienating certain parts of the larger entity. Earlier in this book, I mentioned the Eurovision Song Contest phenomenon. Participants were originally a small group of countries with more or less the same musical taste and culture. Since that time, the contest has matured into a formless – and, according to many, tasteless – music event in which countries form coalitions within their subcultures to select a winner. This inspires a mounting sense of alienation in the original core group.

Britain is a trading nation, a liberal economic nation with great decentralization within its own United Kingdom. The United Kingdom has always been concerned with the trade component but not with the political union that the European Union seeks to create. For the British, Brussels is synonymous with bureaucracy, lack of enterprise, centralism, and profligacy. Of course, the people on the Continent, and especially around Schuman Square in Brussels, take a very different view.

Now that the Brexit genie has been let out of the lamp, fears are growing that other countries in the European Union will follow Britain's example. People repeatedly point at the Netherlands, which in terms of mentality is close to the United Kingdom. But the Dutch are well aware of the importance of export, and Amsterdam is now enjoying big gains from Brexit. So the situation will not change rapidly. Poland has some fundamental conflicts with Europe and would like to see a different relationship. Hungary is drifting away because of its current leadership.

The euro itself has also suffered from major stresses for more than a decade. Greece was narrowly kept in the euro area in 2012, though at the cost of many principles. All partnerships have changed throughout history, so it is certain that new alliances will emerge. Europe, the euro area, the European Free Trade Association, the Schengen Area, the European Union, and NATO (as proved with the Ukrainian conflict) – the composition of these groups of countries changes constantly, but that is not necessarily a problem. There is a good chance that, over the next few decades, some countries will want to leave the euro area or the European Union, and others will want to join. It is not an economic tragedy, but it is a tragedy for certain countries that are forced into an intolerable straitjacket.

In 1992 the United Kingdom left the European Monetary System, the forerunner of the euro area. This was done under pressure from the American-Hungarian speculator and billionaire Georges Soros,[8] who ironically enough today with his Open Society Foundations supports a very pro-European course. Had the British received more support from the German Bundesbank and the other European countries on the continent in 1992, they could have left the European Monetary System in an orderly fashion, or perhaps even stayed in it.[9] Even then, opinion makers predicted that Britain would fall behind economically in the European Union and that London would lose its pre-eminence. Nothing of the sort happened: London became an even more international financial centre and diversified further into other services, something at which Frankfurt and Paris were much less successful.

Small countries also look to their future and their position within the European Union, where they are now dominated by two large countries. Along with seven mainly northern countries, the Netherlands has formed a Hanseatic League, an analogy with the medieval partnership of the same name between the trading cities of roughly the same region. The alliance is a direct outcome of Brexit. The eight small countries fear that Germany and France will no longer be kept in check, now that the (more liberal) United Kingdom has dropped out as a counterweight.

The euro area has suffered the consequences of rapid expansion. Greece was admitted to the euro area on 1 January 2001 for mainly political or geopolitical, rather than economic, reasons – it is a gateway to the East and a NATO member. The country did not meet the accession criteria but could refer to Belgium, for example, which also did not meet that criteria. The implicit aim of the euro area was to counterbalance the US dollar and thus rapidly grow as large as the US currency giant.

The European Union and the euro area are two constellations that were created to engage with globalization: international trade on a global scale between large companies and large power blocs. The European Union would not have expanded as rapidly as it did if trade alone had been the motive. Geopolitical motives played and still play a role. Enlargement to the East is intended to offer a counterweight to Russia and to bind the East European countries to Brussels. At the same time, those countries are given the promise that their economies will converge to Western levels and that their infrastructure and economy will receive a substantial injection of European funds.

China has fundamentally changed the parameters, so much so that we can speak of a period before and a period after December 2001. On 11 December 2001, China joined the World Trade Organization (WTO), after which everything changed. Gigantism was also different before 2001. In 2001 the world welcomed China's accession to the WTO, and companies saw huge opportunities. But because China was given access to Western markets without being obliged to follow the same rules, for example in the social sphere, the game was heavily rigged. Twenty years later these factors play an important role in the countervailing movement that is now underway: deglobalization, the trend whereby economic cohesion in the world decreases and the growth of world trade stagnates.[10] Deglobalization is emerging from the bottom up for the reasons I have already explained. Examples are the yellow vests protests in France and Belgium in 2019, and the outcry against international trade agreements such as CETA. This in turn coincides with the rise of so-called populism in most of the European countries. Politicians and administrators from central government might be slow to notice this movement; they have a personal stake in denying the problem for as long as possible.

Working in Brussels or Washington, one has little sympathy for the industrial workers in Pennsylvania or northern Italy who have been made redundant by globalization. Other jobs are created but not always with the same wages or in the same region. And jobs lost in the creative sectors cannot be replaced by subsidized fake jobs that have no content and cannot arouse any passion in the people who previously loved their work and their community.

There is more to it than protests by the disaffected middle class whose jobs have disappeared. The climate issue forces us to rethink the global economic system. The short chain and localism are gaining popularity. The West has outsourced many of its polluting activities to Eastern Europe, Mexico, or China, but, especially in the latter country, this has resulted in a huge increase in carbon dioxide emissions. Now that pressure to tackle the global problem is building, a reverse movement is gradually underway. Western countries are developing technologies to produce those goods with fewer emissions or to find substitutes. During the COVID-19 pandemic the international logistics chain broke down, and the West also sensed its vulnerabilities. This spurred the urgency to establish more local supplies and production. China, in turn, is also adjusting its politics, moving from an emphasis on exports to greater development of the domestic market. All these phenomena cause the pendulum to swing in the other direction.

Deglobalization is not just an outgrowth of climate plans and the pandemic but, above all, a reaction to gigantism, to the rapid expansion of organizations (World Trade Organization, European Union, and so on), to international agreements that disregard the impact on the local population.

To a large extent, therefore, deglobalization is a healthy movement and will be beneficial for the planet and for society. We must also be careful, however, that the pendulum does not swing too far. The antiglobalists, for example, throw out the baby with the bathwater because globalization offers indisputable benefits. Countries that trade with each other are less likely to go to war. I am a pacifist and believe that many military conflicts are less likely to happen if we provide the right economic incentives for people to trade with each other and thus collaborate economically – especially if this trade includes many small entities and is not seen as a competition between large blocs. That has been the problem with accelerated globalization since 2001, which has become an important factor in the balance of power between the large economic blocs – which also conceal large military interests and forces. The fact that Europe, for example, wants its own army does not seem to me to be a step in the right direction; it would be better to focus on trade and collaboration. Current globalization is thus overshooting its goal. It is no accident that China and the United States are currently engaged in a major trade war. These are conflicts that also rage in cyberspace: control over networks and information is critical. Since the emergence of big tech players in China, the United States has lost its hegemony in that field. Taiwan is now becoming not only a geopolitical pawn but also a core player in the modern technology sector: Taiwan Semiconductors has a 52 per cent global market share in the manufacture of chips. For the United States it is an essential supplier of components for smart phones and computers.

Smaller trade blocs and more balanced relationships can prevent major conflicts. Decentralization not only indicates the direction for globalization 2.0 but also is the means to avoid further deglobalization. A more balanced globalization is feasible if we dare to tackle the current excesses. The pain points of globalization usually concern the loss of jobs and security for a certain segment of the population, social exploitation for another segment, and now, primarily, the climate impacts that we all bear. There is also the feeling that, on the one hand, globalization hugely favours a small elite at the expense of many weaker participants in the world economy. The elite, on the other hand, thinks that today we should mainly fight so-called populism, or fake news. But this is not as simple as it seems. Populism is difficult to define objectively, and it is an often-repeated accusation by political opponents. And fake news can hardly be outlawed and combated in the current Internet age. Both populism and fake news are merely symptoms of the underlying disease, namely that some models have been totally derailed in their pursuit of bigger and more. This fuels the frustration and irritation of large sections of the population, which in turn provides opportunistic politicians with the opportunity to seize power.

The EU model has also run into problems because expansion has occurred too quickly, and too little attention has been paid to subsidiarity. This not only leads to tensions within the European Union but also alienates Europe's top politicians from their populations in the member states. The fake news that, for example, the Russians or others spread about the European Union is then readily swallowed by the already disaffected EU citizens. However, countering such fake news is a hopeless task. It is more important to ensure that the European Union becomes more balanced, less corrupt, and more efficient. In such a European Union, fake news will not easily find fertile ground to germinate.

City-States and Smaller Nations Are the Way Forward for Globalization 2.0

Today globalization is a fact of life, even if its economic organization has derailed. It emphasizes big blocs – China, the United States, the European Union, Japan – but in the future, emphasis will shift to megacities. This is nothing new; throughout history, cities have always been the primary hubs of the great empires. Athens, Sparta, Rome, and Constantinople formed strong local entities in a larger whole. Cities, not the empires, were the true powerhouses, the talent magnets. In his book *The Geography of Genius*,[11] the American author Eric Weiner lists five elements that make cities a magnet for talent and therefore a beacon of economic appeal and prosperity: openness, contrariness, diversity, knowledge, and financial activities. His fundamental insight is that the key to developing ingenuity is openness to innovation and openness to outsiders. Magnets of genius attract talent from afar.

Why is it that the cities, and not the countries, attract the talent? It is difficult to extend some of Weiner's ideas to an entire country without risking that country's becoming unstable. Contrariness, for example, makes it difficult for a country to unite, but it can function in an urban environment. The openness of a city and its citizens, too, is often a typical urban characteristic, as cities are often connected by a river, while the larger entity, the country, remains rather closed. China has never been an open country, although some Chinese port cities do have connections with other cultures and regimes. City-states are merely a state form of the previously discussed decentralization. So, I agree with the Indian-American scientist and best-selling author Parag Khanna, who says that the twenty-first century will not be dominated by China or the United States, but by cities. Cities are becoming islands of good governance in a world that lacks just that. The governance of large entities (United States, European Union) is becoming more unstable for a variety of reasons: corruption, lack of good leadership, alienation, and so on. As a result, cities are becoming the keystones of a new world order. Khanna also emphasizes the role of connectivity between key cities and assumes that such connectivity is easier between cities than between countries. Connectivity is the future, and cities are the nodes of these intra-planetary contacts.[12]

Important cities survive countries and former empires. Rome, Athens, Cairo, and Istanbul retain their prominence although the ancient

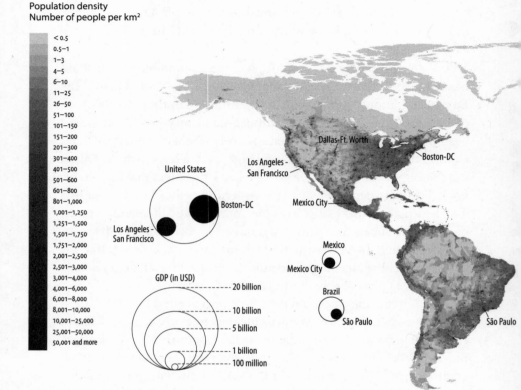

Figure 7.2   Which megacities matter in the world?

Megacities, not nations, are the world's most dominant, sustainable
social structures.

Source: Parag Khanna, https://www.paragkhanna.com/2016-4-21-megacities-not-nations-are-
the-worlds-most-dominant-enduring-social-structures/.

empires to which they belonged have long since disappeared. There are
also no major countries without a major city. Figure 7.2 shows which
megacities hold real importance in the world. The same trend is evident
in Europe (see figure 7.3). Urban networks are a magnet for talent and
for cultural, athletic, and economic activities. It is immediately apparent
that there are a few large urban hubs with millions of inhabitants, but
also that there is a chain of smaller cities with many individual characteristics and differences in relation to each other and the country to which
they belong. The darker clusters are growing, and the lighter ones are
shrinking. Cities are constantly in competition with each other to attract
talent. Dynamic city-states are frequently looking for new activities that

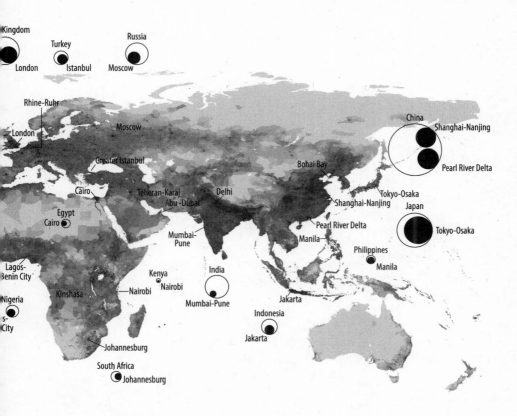

can make them more attractive. Today they are looking for "fintech" players (young companies developing innovative technical products and services for the financial sector) or start-ups in the technology industry, or nowadays the climate industry. In the recent past they targeted trendy fashion and creative activities, and even longer ago, industrialists or bankers. Cities are more flexible than countries in responding swiftly to a new trend. You need not be a member of the European Union to become a thriving city-state. Large cities are magnets in their own right.

At the national level, too, we see that cities perform much better than national entities do. Paris is much better managed than France, London much better than the United Kingdom, and Singapore is a very

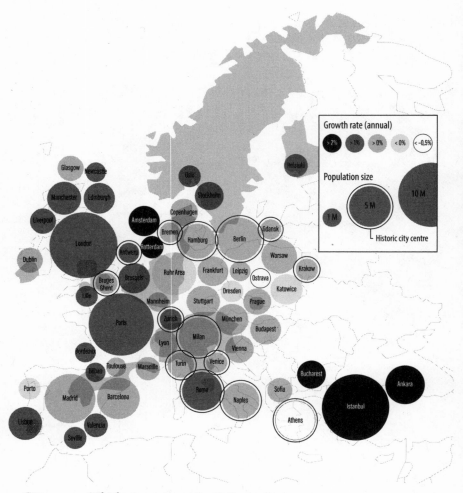

Figure 7.3   Which city-states matter in Europe?
Source: Data based on information from John Donald.

well-managed city-state. Why? A mayor manages to outline a policy
more easily than a president does. City mayors are closer to their population than national or European politicians are, and are quicker to pick
up the pulse of their inhabitants. A mayor's leadership is stronger, which
means that a tighter line can be drawn. Owing to the homogeneous
powers of a mayor and his board of aldermen, decisions are less likely to
be sabotaged or delayed. The link with citizens is stronger, which means
that so-called feedback loops – the rapid evaluation of the implemented

policy, and adjustment if necessary – are shorter. Local policies can respond faster to new needs and insights. During the COVID-19 crisis, cities also appeared to be better governed than countries. Mayors were able to intervene more decisively than ministers. Well-governed cities managed the waves of coronavirus very well, while those countries that were governed poorly went completely off the rails. The list of countries most affected by COVID-19 is thus a good indication of the quality of governance.

Not all cities are successful, however. Some remain trapped in a drab middle ground. There are usually several reasons for this. A city is only really successful if it excels at various levels simultaneously: culture, economy, education, mobility, and leisure. If a city focuses too unilaterally on one domain, it loses out in other areas and fails to become a magnet, and becomes a talent repeller. For example, a city that has a large financial cluster but no cultural attractors or strong academic presence will not be able to compete with London, which has so far succeeded in being a diverse city with excellent cultural, sporting, academic, and historical offerings. Today cities must also invest in state-of-the-art mobility and are challenged to be at the forefront of sustainability and technology. "Smart cities" is the new slogan.

Competition between cities is beneficial to all. The internal struggle between the Italian cities of Rome, Milan, and Turin makes them more creative and prosperous. Switzerland displays strong cohesion, although the internal struggle between, for example, Geneva, Zurich, and Basel is fierce. It is also striking that it is primarily cities – and not countries – that compete to attract entrepreneurial talent. Boston, Berlin, Amsterdam, and London are in the race to attract fintech start-ups. Paris, Milan, New York, and Tokyo vie for fashion talent.

If Europe wants to become more robust, it should not just rely on the Union; it must also draw on the rich diversity found among European cities in order to secure a better place in the global economy. The mix of Europe's rich history and diverse visions for the future of European cities is particularly alluring in a world that increasingly believes that uniformity is the future. However, we must ensure that our cities, too, do not go the way of gigantism.[13]

A successful decentralized network of city-states must allow many more cities to flourish, yet prevent a handful of megacities from becoming a Champions League in their own right. As already pointed out, cities are potentially places where people feel unhappy, so sufficient attention must be paid to different communities and diversity, green spaces, and air quality. New York and London have done very well in this respect, focusing on highly diverse neighbourhoods, mobility plans, and livable city planning.

City-states are, in any case, a step further than the concept that we should form ever-larger blocs. Large entities tend to clash more easily, leading to serious conflicts. The German philosopher Leopold Kohr (1909–1994) also believed this, having lived through two world wars, which convinced him that smaller rather than larger countries should be formed.[14] Today the openness to think about smaller rather than larger political units is taboo. But as Nassim Taleb points out, localism is much more robust in the face of shocks and disruption. Moreover, according to the Lebanese-American scholar, small political units are also better managed: as examples, he cites Cyprus versus Greece (even with the enormous problems since 1974), Singapore versus China and Malaysia, Dubai versus Saudi Arabia, and Switzerland versus Germany.[15] We could also add Luxembourg versus France, and even Iceland versus the European Union; the Icelanders dealt with the bankers better than Europe did.

TEN STEPS TOWARDS POST-GIGANTISM

Healthy capitalism is better than any other system we know. I would like to take humane capitalism and contrast it with today's fake capitalism, which leads to gigantism. Depending on the region, there are more excesses of today's distorted capitalism. The United States has an extreme level of inequality; in Europe the role of the government is too great, which also promotes clientelism, corruption, and crony capitalism; in China there is a variant of state-controlled capitalism that does not take into account the impact on the climate, and the social justice that prevails in the rest of the world. Gigantism is self-destructive because it is far removed from what people want. Various forces, such as technology and human preference, will encourage the growth of smaller organizations that will eventually topple the giants. But this process will take time, and meanwhile the excesses will proliferate. Policy should therefore lend a hand and take targeted measures to speed up the process.

I have compared the economy to a game, so I will continue using this metaphor for a while. If the game is to be played fairly, there must be interventions at every level: the referee, the players, and the rules. Post-gigantism should thus point us towards humane capitalism.

The Referee and the Rules of the Game

It is not a law of the economic system that a few individuals on earth own tens of billions of dollars, and billions of others own only a few tens. It is, however, a consequence of the rules of the game that govern this system and, round after round, shuffle the cards and determine the outcomes. Human beings are being stifled in the current economic system because of an increase in scale and one-dimensional economic thinking and optimization. Perhaps we could start by saying that economists are being trained too one-dimensionally. They are taught that the economy can be modelled, whether through Keynesian is-lm models or through more complex models used today by all kinds of planning agencies and think tanks. They are missing the social aspect and the impact on the environment and the climate. They usually take insufficient account of the generational aspect and what we have come to call sustainability. Economists should therefore study more philosophy and sociology, just as Adam Smith was a philosopher-economist and just as John Maynard Keynes was primarily a mathematician who later became an economist. It explains his penchant for trying to pour economics into formulas and "laws," and perhaps even for believing that economics was a science. So, to be clear, it is not.

Change a few rules, and the economy will function more on a human scale. That is what we need to focus on. Today the rules of the game are designed to encourage bigness. That has not always been the case. As described in detail earlier, many stimuli fuel the growth of structures and encourage them to form larger wholes. Change the incentives, and the economy will behave differently.

A fundamental question is, What should be the basic values of the economic game? Sustainability should be the basic rule of the game. That means that the game is neutral between different generations and does not create social distortions. Furthermore, gigantism places an unnecessarily heavy burden on the environment and the climate, which is of course not intergenerationally neutral. This is largely the result of unbalanced globalization: there are no environmental costs for moving goods around the world, which leads to the development of gigantic logistical networks, whereas increased local production would be far less burdensome on the environment and would also have beneficial social effects.

A game can only be balanced if the referee does not have to intervene or stop it at every turn. Western economies are increasingly becoming planned economies (China always has been). In the West the role of the central planning agency is fulfilled by the central banks, but China has also used that institution more heavily to steer the economy. In principle, central banks are autonomous, but what does that mean today? They are certainly not neutral, and in Europe and the United States these policy instruments have become an extension of the ruling political class and the elite. They were granted this independence at their inception in order for them to be able to intervene in exceptional cases without political interference. But now that they are day traders adjusting the markets, neutrality is no longer an option: when the referee becomes a player, he distorts the game.

To make the economy more balanced, not only the rules of the game have to be changed. The behaviour of the referee and the conditions for the players to participate should also be readjusted. Monopoly-style, I suggest ten adjustments here to make the global economic game fair again.

Referee

The referee must be neutral at all times. This means that he does not take part in the game and has no incentive to favour any particular party.

1   LESS INTERVENTION FROM CENTRAL BANKS

The behaviour of central banks has changed completely since Alan Greenspan became chairman of the US Federal Reserve in 1987. Previously, central bankers only intervened in emergency situations, but that changed dramatically under Greenspan. With his interventionism starting in 1987, and increasing in the years preceding the millennium, investors were beginning to feel that they would always be bailed out by him – like the bank in Monopoly that hands out one hundred notes when a player has overplayed his or her hand. This encouraged bubbles and recklessness. The 1998 rescue of the leveraged fund Long-Term Capital Management, run by Nobel laureates Myron Scholes and Robert C. Merton, further reinforced the sense that the Federal Reserve would always intervene in market panics. As a result, the big players in the financial markets took on more and more risk (which leads to *moral hazard*). Like in a Monopoly game when the rules are no longer followed, it even led to a situation in which those who took the most risk often gained the most.

The transition to a more balanced, sustainable economy is only possible if central banks intervene less and allow the financial markets to do their job. Players who take too much risk, and fail as a result, will then be pushed out of the economy, making room for more cautious, responsible players. When financial markets operate normally, fear of losing money creeps into the system, followed by higher-risk premiums. This, in turn, has the effect of reducing the risks and levers that businesses will use – mostly debt, but there are other possibilities – to make themselves bigger than they could naturally be. Central banks are the dealers of money steroids, which are mainly used by the biggest players. SMES are less likely to get into the dealer circuit.

2   NOT "TOO BIG TO FAIL"

Large organizations that fail must be dismantled in an orderly manner. No single organization should be too big to fail. If that is the case, the government should nationalize that company in the event of bankruptcy. In 2008 it was mainly the large banks in large European countries that were spared. I have observed the same behaviour in other sectors in the past: steel companies, car manufacturers, and shipyards were kept alive by the government for too long. Today we face the risk in yet other sectors, as the climate transition stimulates new models and new players. When a large tree falls, it creates light and oxygen for hundreds of smaller plants. The referee should not be intimidated by a big player. If that player has to be sent off, then so be it, even if it is Lionel Messi, Cristiano Ronaldo, or Mbappé.

3   SUBSIDIARITY: DECENTRALIZE WHEN POSSIBLE

The European Union is built on the principle of subsidiarity, yet this principle is not very well known. Subsidiarity means that decisions should be made at the lowest possible level (i.e., as close as possible to the citizen). If it is better for a decision to be made at municipal, cantonal, or provincial level, then that would be preferable.

Large corporations would rather that decisions were made centrally because they have more control over them. Large governments deal more easily with large companies. That is why the principle of subsidiarity is so important to ensure that the rules of the game remain fair for both large and small companies. So if there is a choice between a local or an international referee, it is best to choose the former in order to make the game more democratic and sustainable.

Rules of the Game

The rules of the game are formulated by competent experts, with sufficient diversity, who have an eye for the general interest and the fairness of the outcome, and who themselves also wish to be judged on the results.

4   CLOSE LOOPHOLES, INCREASE CORPORATE INCOME TAX AT INTERNATIONAL LEVEL, AND MAKE NO DISTINCTION BETWEEN MULTINATIONAL COMPANIES AND SMES

The past forty years have been one long downhill slide for corporate tax. Large companies in particular have enjoyed steadily declining tax rates, partly due to the international "beauty contests" to lure these large corporations to a specific location. Large multinational companies have enough specialists and consultants on board who can help them identify the least taxed path, but small and local companies cannot avail themselves of these tax shortcuts, so they usually pay the full price. The discrepancy between large and small, and the many loopholes for multinational companies, can only be eliminated through international cooperation and an ethical attitude from all the companies' stakeholders. The minimum tax of 15 per cent for international companies that the OECD recently managed to obtain is thus a genuinely important measure. If everything goes as planned, multinationals will be obliged to pay a minimum of 15 per cent tax in the countries in which their offices are located, from 2023 onwards. Escape routes via existing tax havens such as the British Virgin Islands or Panama will no longer be an option.

The referees also need to have the backbone to exclude cheaters. In the major banks numerous players who organized tax fraud have been caught in recent years. They would usually be handed a red card and be excluded for several years. If big players enjoy tax breaks as well as preferential treatment from the referee, the game can never be fair.

5   STRICTER ANTITRUST LAWS

The capitalist game has become one of cartels, oligarchs, near-monopolists, and guilds,[1] with all kinds of barriers to entry, such as quality, safety, and often unnecessary training. In fact, one can no longer even speak of capitalism, but of an organized form of protected benefits or rent-seeking.[2]

To make the economic game fairer, therefore, the referees must apply stricter antitrust rules. This should not be done in one region, as is currently the case in Europe, but across all regions simultaneously. Otherwise, there will be even more distortions, and a "prisoner's dilemma" will be created: the countries that play the game fairly will never win against those that cheat.

Not only should US tech giants Facebook, Google, Microsoft, Apple, and Amazon be subject to strict antitrust rules, but the same should apply to Chinese tech companies. Right now, China is copying the United States, but in an extra-extra-large version. China's size is a factor to be feared, and because antitrust law in that country depends on the arbitrariness of the Communist Party, China's economic policy also distorts the global economic game. In future our governments must therefore exercise more critical supervision when Chinese companies begin to take over our economies. After all, reciprocity is virtually impossible. Chinese companies that use state capital to acquire an oligopoly on Western markets pose a threat to free competition and fair economic play.

6   BAN TAKEOVERS BY GIGACORPORATIONS

Some of today's football giants have enough players to form three first-division teams. This kills creative talent, but, most of all, it keeps the competition small. Potential competitors can never rise to their level and pose a genuine threat. For exactly the same reason, the tech giants buy up small promising technology players even before they can pose a material threat. Mergers and acquisitions, in other words, have become a factor that limits not only competition but also innovation.

Just as the football associations FIFA and UEFA try to develop a fair play rule for football transfers and ensure that football clubs remain financially healthy (for example, too much debt is not permitted), international bodies and national governments should prevent large companies from simply buying up promising companies. A ban on M&A may sound crazy in today's financial culture, but if we look at the number and size of M&A transactions in the recent past, one cannot help but conclude that the current buying frenzy is in fact crazy.

It is unlikely that such a measure will be given the green light any time soon; the lobby of the big corporations and their advisors (who make big money out of such transactions) will do all they can to prevent the passing of such laws. When you see how many alumni of Goldman

Sachs and other investment banks are now serving in governments, lobbying organizations, and international bodies, you know that there is still a long way to go. But it is the road we have to travel to restore a healthy, balanced economy.

7   CO$_2$ TAX ON INTERNATIONAL TRANSPORT AND, IDEALLY, ALSO ON EMISSIONS PRODUCED BY INTERNATIONAL PRODUCTION PROCESSES

It has been my hobby horse for more than ten years: a fair environmental tax must be levied on the external costs of the global logistics networks and international production. By *external costs* I mean the environmental damage, safety risks, and negative social consequences of the worldwide transport of goods and services. Please note that this is not a call to stop globalization or to join the antiglobalists. It is, however, a necessary corollary to increased international trade and cooperation. If international networks are free, then only economic optimization takes place. If goods are produced in a more polluting manner far away but can still be imported more cheaply, local consumers have to realize that they must also pay for the pollution that they have indirectly caused far away. Relocating basic production has reduced emissions in the West since 1990, but the footprint of Western consumers has increased as a result.

If other external costs are included, the economy will still optimize, but it will also take into account the social and ecological costs and opportunities. As a result, local production will have greater opportunities: production will be more competitive if these costs are included. Another consequence is that some sectors will no longer be dominated by globally active mastodons, and local diversity will flourish and have a chance again. Finally, such a climate tax would also curb the gigantism of logistics. Perhaps this will lead to more human-scale logistics networks that are small-scale and decentralized, as well as to more local production.

Although my reflection on the CO$_2$ tax is mainly motivated by the far-reaching consequences of gigantism, my concern for the climate also plays a major role. I have always criticized the climate agreement signed in Paris in 2015 because it did not provide for such a CO$_2$ tax on international transport.[3] Indeed, it is impossible to seriously reduce CO$_2$ emissions without such a tax.

Players

The players respect the rules of the game, refrain from actively influencing the referee, and are penalized for unfair behaviour – with expulsion, if necessary.

8   ACCEPT GLOBAL SOCIAL RULES

No game can be sustainable if the players themselves do not demonstrate or embrace a sustainable attitude. Economists have a highly theoretical and mechanical view of international trade. It is always positive for all players: the more trade, the better. They always mention comparative advantages in their models. What economists neglect to mention, however, is that they invariably assume that all players accept the same rules. These rules are not purely economic, but are also social. Child labour, exploitation of employees, and other social abuses are the order of the day in today's global economy. We turn a blind eye to them because we believe we are in a transitional period.

Indeed, millions of Chinese were lifted out of poverty by free trade. If we had imposed our social rules on China, no world trade agreement would have been signed in 2001. But about twenty years have passed, and we need to take a more stringent approach. Stricter rules against child labour, strict safety standards for staff, the admission of trade unions, or serious legal protection of workers: these are rules that China and many other "emerging" economies could have accepted by now. They have had enough time to do so but were not put under enough pressure. Large multinationals usually only react when it is conclusively proven that their subcontractors do not abide by the legal rules. But proactive action to prevent abuses is insufficient.

Without minimum social standards, countries and companies should not be allowed to participate in the international economic game. Otherwise, those countries that do comply with social rules will be at a competitive disadvantage vis-à-vis the freebooters, and eventually the cheaters will drive the fair players out of the game. That can never be the purpose of a game based on fair play.

9   EXCLUSION OR LONG-TERM SUSPENSION FOR CHEATERS

Any game can only end well if one has the courage to exclude cheaters. In the economic game no one has the nerve. The rules are sometimes too vague or not strict enough, and there are no referees, or the referees are too often semi-players. Above all, the cheaters are big and feel untouchable. One of the reasons why penalties are usually light or not handed down or enforced is that international trade has the aura of "always good" and "whatever you do, don't obstruct it." As previously mentioned, economists mistake this for not taking other dimensions into account. As a result, players still abide by the strictly economic rules of the game – for example, no price fixing, no aggressive dumping practices, and compliance with local economic legislation – but all the rules that are not purely economic are simply flouted.

China cheats on intellectual property rights and disregards many Western social rights. Even basic human rights do not count in that country. The United States has not adhered to the Paris climate agreement, but now under President Biden it seems to want to make more effort. American companies are permitted to make acquisitions in all countries, but, conversely, national security is readily invoked. Nor is Europe sacrosanct; for example, it does not allow African producers to export their food products freely to Europe, allegedly for quality reasons. Russian oligarchs have different business ethics than Western companies have, but it has been impossible to take action against them (until the war in Ukraine started). Brazil is allowed to destroy the Amazon rainforest to optimize its agriculture, without any trade sanctions. Saudi Arabia fails to respect human rights and bombs its neighbour Yemen, and yet it participates in world trade without a hitch.

International trade should be reserved for fair players – both countries and companies. This has nothing to do with protectionism but with protecting sustainability; it would benefit the planet and local people. Therefore, if we want to protect people, communities, and the planet from cheating, we will have to raise our standards and be tougher on offenders.

10   DISTANCE BETWEEN PLAYERS, REFEREES, AND REGULATORS

The term *crony capitalism* stands for an economy in which success or failure is not the result of risk-taking, innovation, or entrepreneurship but the result of companies' ties to the political class. This crony capitalism has now reached problematical proportions in just about all capitalist countries, and the ties are often so close that nobody questions them anymore.

Take the example of revolving-door politics, a term that refers to the practice whereby high-ranking politicians, upon expiry of their political mandate, end up in the first echelon of the business world. Former German chancellor Gerhard Schröder not only obtained a top job at the Russian oil and gas company Gazprom after his political career, but also was appointed to the board of the Swiss investment bank Rothschild. Former president of the European Commission José Manuel Barroso quickly moved to the investment bank Goldman Sachs. And the Dutch former European commissioner for competition Neelie Kroes became head of the important advisory board of the taxi company Uber and a special advisor at Bank of America Merrill Lynch.

Career moves between the political and the private sphere are not necessarily bad, but they can lead to a conflict of interests: the forester who becomes a poacher is more familiar with places in which there are few controls (which is not to say that private companies are all poachers). A cooling-off period of at least twelve months would be a great help, but some jobs should remain off limits even after that. The best thing would be to agree on this clearly in advance.

Another example is the numerous summits at which politicians and top managers meet. Most of these events are out of reach for the local entrepreneur or the CEO of a small multinational. The World Economic Forum in Davos, Switzerland, is one of the best-known examples, along with the even more exclusive Bilderberg Conference. Politics and business are also strongly intertwined during trade missions – not to mention the numerous events organized by all kinds of lobby groups, where politics and business like to make an appearance. In itself, this is not necessarily a bad thing. The exchange of insights is potentially highly beneficial for both sides; however, there is also a great danger in these kinds of meetings – an elite club is created of influential policy-makers and CEOs drawn mainly from the largest companies.

The world view of these CEOs will be greatly distorted by one-sided contacts with only part of the economic world, and lobbying is never far away. For example, it became apparent that the Davos Summit in 2017 had a profound influence on the migration agreements signed in Marrakech in 2018.[4] Large companies have a vested interest in ensuring that there is an adequate supply of cheap labour. The World Economic Forum in Davos is always the leading advocate of international trade without barriers, but the bubble in the Swiss Alps creates an artificial atmosphere that leads politicians to believe that all economic measures that pass the Davos test must automatically benefit everyone.

I would therefore argue for more distance between politicians and CEOs and at least better governance of those contacts. Increasingly, one can follow the Davos presentations publicly; the list of participants can be found with a little snooping. But that is not the point. Privileged close contacts are developing between a small club of large companies and organizations and a small (but frequently changing) group of crucial policy-makers. None of those large multinationals would be able to connect with a newly elected president within a year without the annual World Economic Forum in Davos. This is not as innocent as it seems. The summit in the Swiss winter resort naturally provides a superb program, with scores of interesting presentations and debates, which is the perfect reason for many top leaders to make the trip to the snowy mountains. However, it is not the content that is of paramount importance to them, but the preferential contacts and the opportunities for exerting influence that can arise. This is what the giant companies are after, and this justifies the extravagant cost of a few days in Davos.[5]

The Bilderberg conferences are even more exclusive and secret. In fact, they balance on the edge of what is democratically acceptable because they bring together an elite group from the business world with a select number of political leaders and highly placed members of influential policy organizations. This kind of invitation-only, backroom politics also creates an ideal breeding ground for a variety of action groups and even conspiracy theorists.

It would really be quite something if this elite, the media, and the democratic organizations were to realize that Davos, Bilderberg, and other clubs created by the Goldman Sachses and Rothschilds of this world were capable of disrupting the economic game.

Saving Capitalism from Fake Capitalists

It would not hurt if decision makers gave some thought to these ten solutions. If I had to rank the proposals according to their greatest impact, the order would be slightly different. Suppose the world leaders asked me to reform the economic game, where would I start? What is the feasibility of the proposed measures?

DAVOS: THE PRICE OF EXCLUSIVITY

The more expensive you make something, the more exclusive it becomes. Davos understood that very well. In 2011 the *New York Times* calculated the price of a few days of networking in the mountains:[6]

- It starts with a compulsory annual membership in the World Economic Forum. In 2011 such a membership card cost about USD 52,000. An industry partner pays USD 263,000, and a strategic partner USD 527,000. Each membership level confers different privileges.
- Then there is the cost of an entrance ticket for the conference itself, for which one paid at least USD 19,000 in 2011, excluding taxes.
- To have access to the private sessions – where the really exclusive encounters take place – one has to become an industry associate at a cost of USD 137,000 per year.
- To bring a colleague, one must become an industry partner and upgrade the membership: USD 263,000. This colleague also pays USD 19,000 in entrance fees.
- To bring a group of colleagues, one is required to become a strategic partner (USD 527,000) and to buy five entrance tickets for the price of USD 19,000 each. At least one of the five invited colleagues must be a woman.

One can only become a strategic partner if one belongs to the world's 250 largest companies. Of course, then you only have access to Davos and its conferences. There are also many other costs. The winter sports resort is very expensive anyway, but during the conference week the hotels there are unaffordable for ordinary mortals. The smallest backroom cannot be booked for less than USD 500 a night. The cost of a chalet is USD 150,000 dollars for a week.

Invoices quickly run into the millions to get into the annual World Economic Forum. The fact that companies cough up such sums every year may have something to do with the content of the presentations, but since these lectures can nowadays also be followed for free by ordinary people, one might suspect that it has to do with other things as well.

My personal top three urgent measures are as follows:

1 Tighten antitrust measures.
2 End inappropriately close contact between the corporate world and politics (crony capitalism).
3 Introduce a worldwide CO_2 tax on international transport (shipping and aviation).

Table 8.1   Feasibility of post-gigantism, step by step

Step	Measure	Impact on gigantism	Feasibility
1	Less intervention by central banks	8	–
2	No longer too big to fail	6	=
3	Subsidiarity: decentralize where possible	4	+
4	Close loopholes and raise corporate tax internationally, and no tax differential between multinationals and SMES	7	+
5	Tighten antitrust laws	1	+
6	Ban takeovers by giga corporations	5	–
7	CO_2 tax on international transport	3	+
8	Accept social rules	9	+
9	Exclusion or long-term suspension for cheats	10	–
10	Combat crony capitalism	2	+

These three measures will have an enormous impact not only on gigantism but also on society, the environment, and the climate. They are the three most urgent measures if we want to save capitalism and put an end to the current abuse of the capitalist rules of play.

Not that the other steps are unimportant. On the contrary. But if we want to have an impact quickly, it is best to start with the biggest levers. The debate on central bank policy, for example, is complex; moreover, central banks insist on their independence from politics. I would strongly encourage the prohibition of takeovers by giant companies, but the Champions League in football teaches us that large clubs pay little attention to commissions relating to financial fair play and steadfastly continue to plunder the world's talent from smaller clubs. The social rules must also be respected and intensified, but, for all manner of reasons, many are afraid to demand this of China and the other emerging economies, for example.

Let us be optimistic: the pressure to change the system has intensified in recent years, with the OECD's minimum tax and the Biden administration's criticism of certain tech giants as early signs of a new spring. The coronavirus pandemic has heightened social awareness and demonstrated that globalization must and can be different. So there are moves afoot, which will be further stimulated by the more stringent climate ambitions.

Capitalism is usually defended by the people and organizations who today benefit from its current derailed form. These are the rent-seekers, as they were first called by economist Anne Krüger in 1974 after a theory advanced by Gordon Tullock in 1967. Obviously, those who benefit from the systems that lead to rent-seeking will not change the system. However, the adherents of Adam Smith's philosophy – the defenders of humane capitalism – are few and far between. The neo-capitalism that many (rightly) vilify has little in common with the original ideas of the founding fathers of the economic liberalism that Smith espoused.

As so many people and organizations benefit from the system, change is painful and slow. Thus, true change only happens during major crises or when the old system finally implodes. However, world history shows that in that chaos and anarchy, ordinary citizens are once again the losers. For this reason it is in our interest to take to heart the ideas and solutions that have been put forward. We must save capitalism from abuse by fake capitalists.

CONCLUSIONS

"Aren't we living in great times and having tremendous comfort?" Surely the marvels of technology have spread far and wide, transforming our lives for the better? Surely the Champions League delivers spectacular football, the like of which we have never seen? Isn't the way we have built huge organizations amazing? Why do we suddenly need to worry about things becoming too large when they also deliver a host of benefits?

Prosperity has certainly increased enormously over the last forty years, and we can look forward to better health, longer life expectancy, and less poverty overall. But this should not blind us to the enormous challenges we face, challenges that are acute because we failed to take a more preventive approach and did not adequately shockproof our economy and society. Gigantism is not immune to shocks; it is extremely vulnerable, as the *Ever Given* painfully demonstrated in 2021 by blocking the Suez Canal and, in doing so, wreaking havoc on the world economy. If, a few decades ago, we had conceived of an economic model that calculated the full costs for all generations, not simply the current costs, the climate crisis would not exist today. Globalization has conferred disproportionate advantages on "being big," displacing local, smaller-scale activities and leaving larger, international organizations to take the biggest slice of the pie.

How has it come to this? Surely no one should be surprised that we have reached this point after the policies of the past decades. Those policies aimed at achieving economic growth, and, more than once, the reaction of the stock markets was a benchmark of success. This is defensible but misses an important complement: is this growth socially just? Do the profits and the development of some companies serve the interests of society? Economics cannot be separated from morality, that is, acting and behaving well, in line with one's conscience and the prevailing norms and values.

Morality, therefore, is not simply something to be explored by philosophers or by those with a spiritual or religious inclination. It must be an integral part of economic or other policies. The word *morality* is derived from the Latin word *mos*, which means "rule." It is usually used in the plural: *mores*. Thus it means the morals, habits, or rules we have accepted as the basis of our society. Teaching someone mores is not just teaching them a lesson. Economic policy must follow the mores and reward virtuous behaviour, and penalize immoral behaviour by curbing it economically or even making it impossible. It is therefore an interplay between morality and economics. It is also closely related to the aspect of fairness, just as fair play is important in a game.

This is precisely why Adam Smith's philosophy is so compelling: his second work (*An Inquiry into the Wealth of Nations*, 1776) should not be viewed independently of his first book (*Theory of Moral Sentiments*, 1759). Economics is not only about pursuing self-interest but also about ensuring that that self-interest is in harmony with the common good or, better still, reinforces the common good. In his first book Adam Smith spoke of the "impartial spectator," an independent observer of our actions who addresses us on their morality.[1] One could also call it "a conscience." It is no small matter and is essential for leaders in whom we must have confidence.

In *The Wealth of Nations* Adam Smith speaks a different, harsher language for some. The story of the baker is a familiar example: "It is not from the benevolence of the butcher, the brewer, or the baker, that we expect our dinner, but from their regard to their own interest. We address ourselves, not to their humanity but to their self-love, and never talk to them of our own necessities but of their advantages."[2] That sounds rather harsh, as though to all intents and purposes, in terms of economic transactions, pure self-interest is the only thing that counts. However, we should bear in mind that *The Wealth of Nations* and *The Theory of Moral Sentiments* must be considered as a whole; they are two sides of the same coin that steers our society in the right direction.

The customer who drops in at the bakery expects to see shelves of wholesome, tasty bread. The baker does not sell bread out of the goodness of his heart but because it serves his personal interests; it is to his advantage. In Adam Smith's world, there is no monopoly, and the customer is free to take her custom elsewhere. In Adam Smith's world, the baker cannot make a deal with the local or higher government to overcharge for poor quality bread, or to be the only one allowed to supply bread to the government or its associates. This world has rights and obligations and is driven by fairness. A baker who bakes the best bread in the village will have a longer queue of customers at his door. The other bakers will have to find another strategy, such as baking cakes or retraining. The difference lies in the popularity of his bread, not in his position of power. Every day, customers will keep an eye on the quality of his loaves, but loyal customers will help him to improve his product, too. It is a fair deal.

Adam Smith's world is finely tuned to include self-interest and public interest; competition and fairness; a competitive advantage but opportunities for others; anticipation of new things, (i.e., innovation); and personal risk as well as solidarity. In the world of gigantism, things are very different. The bakery chain is controlled centrally; the baker operates the cash register but is not involved in the production process. The customer has chosen this branch of Big Bakery Ltd. because it is reliable, convenient, or cheap. Or because it has outlets at all the right locations, making it difficult for other bakers to set up shop there. Or perhaps the bakery chain has moved into the city, first driving out local bakeries by undercutting prices, then altering the quality of the bread and the price. This limits customers' choice, and new bakers think twice before, like David, they attempt to take on Goliath. If the government wants to promote bread, it is easier to negotiate with the big chain than with all those local bakers. Of course, it also works the other way around, because the CEO of the large bakery group is a welcome guest in political circles or on foreign governmental missions.

There is also another important aspect. What if things go awry? If the local bakery bakes a batch of tainted loaves and, in the worst-case scenario, someone dies, that baker goes out of business. And there is room for a new bakery. If that happens to a bakery chain, the consequences are more widely felt. The impact is far greater. But there is a different, more important point. The local baker eats his own bread; he knows whether it is good or bad. If he cannot talk to his customers about his products, there is no trust. If things go wrong, chances are he is the first to get sick from the contaminated bread. He knows all his customers, and they will soon turn up at his door, complaining. But there is a greater distance between a large bakery chain and the customer. Personal contact is non-existent, and he hardly knows the end customers. All the strengths of decentralized systems for society come to the surface: greater diversity, less risk, personal responsibility, more fairness, and so on.

Should the bad baker be subsidized? No. Is that unfair? Not at all. He should eat his own bread and talk to his customers. Should the government bail out the big bakery chain when it fails? No, it should not. Is that unfair to the staff? No. It would only be unfair if they were compensated by the government, and the staff at the ordinary bakery were not compensated for the same. Smith's logic is not purely economic; it is a balance between morality and fair competition, in which self-interest serves the common good.

How this morality be instilled at a higher level and in bigger organizations? Here, the choice of leaders is imperative. Their moral fortitude must at least match the other traits that qualify them for the job. Today, that does not happen nearly enough. Take the example of Christine Lagarde, who is currently president of the European Central Bank, despite being convicted in the Bernard Tapie case while she was still working at the International Monetary Fund. Lagarde was found guilty of negligence because she had failed to lodge a government appeal against the payment of EUR 400 million to Tapie. She could have faced a prison sentence and a fine, but because of her good reputation and the fact that she was fighting a global financial crisis at the time, she was not penalized. However, the fact that she was later appointed to an even more important role, with enormous social responsibilities, is not acceptable.

Leaders of prominent organizations must demonstrate impeccable moral conduct. Unfortunately the list of morally questionable individuals in key institutions and positions is long. Donald Trump lacks the moral authority required of an American president, but unfortunately there have been other examples in recent decades. Michel Platini and Sepp Blatter are examples of amoral leaders in the world of football, and between 2000 and 2019, governance at the IMF was compromised. These are significant examples. When selecting top leaders, we attach too little importance to their morality and too much to their (perceived) charisma. Morally strong leaders with little charisma should always be favoured over the reverse.

It does not stop there. Moral responsibility cannot always be imposed, but financial accountability can. Leaders who fail through recklessness, corruption, personal enrichment, and incompetence should feel it. An architect should live beneath his bridge or use it every day. Hedge fund managers should put all their savings into their fund, not a few symbolic dollars. A banker should repay his bonuses if the bank fails. The politician who proves to be corrupt should lose his financial and other privileges. This is called "skin in the game." The baker who bakes bad bread loses his past and his future, even if he did so unintentionally. The consequences for the "little guy" are more direct than for the captain of our gigantic ships.

If we want to break away from gigantism, we will have to do more than just change the rules of play; we will have to rediscover the import-ance of morality, the gravitas of leaders, and the good governance of our organizations. The latter is not a technicality; it is fundamental. According to economists Daron Acemoglu and James Robinson, inclusive, diverse organizations make the difference between successful and failing nations.[3] Adam Smith would have approved of their ideas. Such organizations will keep the distance between business and politics healthy and therefore sufficiently large, and elect moral leaders to govern them. If we look at all our organizations and leaders through this lens, we see that there is a considerable amount of room for improvement and that we need to be tougher on our leaders if they show any signs of corruption. The morality of our leaders determines the fairness that we can expect in our society.

Our future lies in embracing old, tried-and-tested ideas to build a fair society, sound leadership, and a vibrant economy where progress, innovation, and collective success are the product of morally driven, ambitious individuals who use their talents for the betterment of all, not just themselves.

Long live humane capitalism! Long live Adam Smith!

EPILOGUE

In December 2019 a planned merger between two educational institutions in the Belgian university town of Leuven was called off. The protesters cited *Gigantisme: Van too big to fail naar trager, kleiner en menselijke* and the pernicious influence of scale on education and educational performance. I am extremely proud of that. I hope that more and more people will learn to appreciate the importance of smaller organizations. We must cherish the "wolves" in our society, who increase diversity and ultimately slow down and improve the flow of our rivers.

I would like to thank the following people for their valuable input in bringing this book to fruition: Gertjan Verdickt, En Hua Hu, Jolien Noels, Maarten Van Steenbergen, Jan Lodewyckx, Jan Peter Balkenende, Erik Weiner, Pattie Maes, Barry Ritholtz, Parag Khanna, Paul Hawken, Caro, Johan Van Overtveldt, Joël De Ceulaer, and at McGill-Queen's University Press, Kathleen Fraser, Carol Bonnett, Jennifer Roberts, and Jacqueline Davis.

NOTES

Chapter One

1 Heede, "Tracing Anthropogenic Carbon Dioxide"; Griffin, Carbon Majors Database: CDP Carbon Majors Report 2017.
2 r > g, whereby r = return on capital, g = economic growth.
3 Seeking a political interest, a return with no real risk, and a return with no added value for society.
4 See http://citeseerx.ist.psu.edu/viewdoc/download?doi=10.1.1.730.3483 &rep=rep1&type=pdf.
5 Phelps, *Corporatism and Keynes*.
6 Von Hayek was also an opponent of monopolies and oligopolies.
7 McCloskey, *The Bourgeois Virtues*; *Bourgeois Dignity*; *Bourgeois Equality*.
8 See Tobias Helmersson et al., "Corporate Zombification: Post-Pandemic Risks in the Euro Area," Financial Stability Review, May 2021, https://www.ecb.europa.eu/pub/financial-stability/fsr/special/html/ecb.fsrart202105 _01~f9b060744e.en.html.
9 Kohr, *The Breakdown of Nations*, 13.
10 Illich, *Deschooling Society*.
11 Mazzucato, *Mission Economy*; Mazzucato, "Stop Whining about Big Government."
12 Kelton, *The Deficit Myth*; Kelton, "How We Think about the Deficit."
13 Krugman, "What's Wrong with Functional Finance?"; and Paul Krugman (@paulkrugman), "Stephanie Kelton responds – and I feel a sense of despair 1/," Twitter thread, 1 March 2019, 3:41 p.m., https://twitter.com/paulkrugman/status/1101583214714474503.
14 DP *Carbon Majors Report, 2017*, The Carbon Majors Database, https://cdn.cdp.net/cdp-production/cms/reports/documents/000/002/327/original/Carbon-Majors-Report-2017.pdf?1501833772.

Chapter Two

1 Manyika, Birshan, Smit, Woetzel, Russell, and Purcell, "A New Look."
2 The size of a company cannot be determined by one parameter. Some companies have tens of thousands of employees but have relatively little significance in the global economy. Others achieve a turnover of billions of dollars, but, if this is the result of transit (import/export), their added value may be negligible. Market capitalization takes into account both the added value and a company's future development (as opposed to turnover or the number of employees today), but it can be inflated (referred to as "bubbles") and fluctuates by at least 25 per cent per year anyway. Thus, it is better to use several parameters to determine "big," but market capitalization is the only parameter that also takes the future of the company into account.
3 Leonhardt, "The Charts."
4 Big companies have always existed, but, converted into today's dollars, the giants of the past are dwarves compared to today's (listed) companies. That is not to say that gigantism was not a problem in the past, only that the problem is much more acute today.
5 Quentin Peel, "Merkel Warns on Cost of Welfare," *Financial Times*, 16 December 2012, https://www.ft.com/content/ 8cc0f584-45fa-11e2-b7ba-00144feabdco.
6 Ritholtz, "Apple Becomes the Largest Company Ever."
7 Giancotti, Guglielmo, and Mauro, "Efficiency and Optimal Size of Hospitals," *PLOS ONE* 12, no. 3: e01733.
8 Bordo and Jonung, "The Future of Emu."
9 Bouman, "De wal keert het schip."
10 Levinson, *The Box*, cited in Bouman, "De wal keert het schip."
11 Grullon, Larkin, and Michaely, "Are U.S. Industries Becoming More Concentrated?"
12 Veugelers, "Are European Firms Falling Behind?"
13 Döttling, Gallardo, and Philippon, T. "Is There an Investment Gap in Advanced Economies?"
14 The evidence rested on tracking average markups on goods and services provided by listed companies in 74 countries. This is the extent to which a company can bump up its prices relative to its costs, being an obvious and simple measure of its power in the market. See Diez, Leigh, and Tambunlertchai, "Global Market Power."
15 Autor, Dorn, Katz, Patterson, and Van Reenen, "The Fall of the Labor Share."
16 Salinas, "Amazon Raises Minimum Wage." Miles, Borchert, and Ramanathan, "Why Some Merging Companies Become Synergy."

17 An increase in the number of *corporate structures* is not necessarily the same
    as an increase in the number of *companies*. Fiscal structures or privatization
    of employees are two important examples of this.

Chapter Three

1 Miles, Borchert, and Ramanathan, "Why Some Merging Companies Become
   Synergy Overachievers."
2 Lewis and McKone, "So Many M&A Deals Fail," 1–5.
3 Nguyen and Kleiner, "The Effective Management of Mergers," 447–54.
4 Johansson, Skeie, Sorbe, and Menon, "Tax Planning by Multinational Firms."
5 According to Professor James A. Thurber, Department of Government,
   School of Public Affairs, American University, Washington.
6 Sherman Anti-Trust Act, 2 July 1890; Enrolled Acts and Resolutions of
   Congress, 1789–1992; General Records of the United States Government;
   Record Group 11; National Archives, https://www.archives.gov/milestone-
   documents/sherman-anti-trust-act.
7 Gutiérrez and Philippon, "How EU Markets Became More Competitive Than
   US Markets."

Chapter Four

1 Calculations by Jolien Noels and En Hua Hu, based on the database of
   Bert Kassies.
2 FC Barcelona estimates that more than 10,000 tourists come to the Spanish
   city for each home match.
3 Real Madrid, FC Barcelona, Manchester United, Bayern Munich, Chelsea,
   Arsenal, Juventus, Paris Saint-Germain, Manchester City, Liverpool, and
   AC Milan.
4 Atlético Madrid, Borussia Dortmund, Olympique Marseille, Inter Milan,
   and AS Roma.
5 Cunningham, Ederer, and Ma, "Killer Acquisitions."
6 Cunningham, Ederer, and Ma, "Killer Acquisitions."
7 Jessica Naziri, "Wal-Mart, Unions Reach Tentative Deal for Possible NYC
   Stores," CNN, 4 February 2011, http://edition.cnn.com/2011/US/02/03/new.
   york.walmart/index.html.
8 Angotti, Paul, Gray, and Williams, *Wal-mart's Economic Footprint*.

Chapter Five

1 Bed Bath and Beyond, Albertson, Walgreens, cvs Caremark, Lowe's, Best Buy, Safeway, Publix, Macy's, Dollar General, The Gap, Sears, Costco, Kroger, Home Depot, Target, and so on.

2 *Columbia Magazine*, "What Do Retail Workers Want?"

3 *Journal of Commerce*, "JOC Top 100 US Importer and Exporter Rankings, 2020," https://www.joc.com/joc-top-100-us-importer-and-exporter-rankings-2020_20210525.htm.

4 Alliance for American Manufacturing, "Fact Sheet: Walmart's Made in America Pledge," 2016, https://www.americanmanufacturing.org/press-release/fact-sheet-walmarts-made-in-america-pledge.

5 Jia, "What Happens When Wal-Mart Comes to Town."

6 Courtemanche and Carden, "Supersizing Supercenters?"

7 Wolfe and Pyrooz, "Rolling Back Prices and Raising Crime Rates?" Lead author Scott Wolfe, assistant professor of criminology at the University of South Carolina, examined counties where Walmart expanded and compared them with counties where it did not. The decline in crime rates stopped in counties where Walmart expanded in the 1990s. The study examined annual crime rates in 3,109 counties between 1991 and 2009. Wolfe focused in particular on the 1990s, when the national crime rate fell sharply and Walmart expanded rapidly. The study found evidence that the decline in crime slowed in counties where Walmart emerged, and the trend continued after the year 2000. Counties were adjusted for poverty, unemployment, immigration, population structure, and residential changes, among other factors, so that the scientists could isolate the Walmart effect. In December 2019, six months after the first edition of *Capitalism XXL*, a remarkable report appeared in the *New York Times*: "The Town That Lost Its Walmart," about Edna, a small town in Texas. Six months earlier, Walmart had announced that it was closing its stores there. This was an enormous shock for the local community: it came as a demotion, and people feared losing jobs, incomes, and residents. "Case studies and books have examined what happens to a community when a Walmart muscles in, how the retailer uses its enormous leverage to lower prices and undercut competitors. But less has been said about what happens when Walmart suddenly packs up and leaves." (See Corkery, "The Town That Lost Its Walmart.") So it was a real-time event that could show the reverse impact of Walmart. It turned out to be not that bad: the reverse of the effects of the "De Blasio report" on Wal-mart's Economic Footprint (see Angotti et al., *Wal-mart's Economic Footprint*) (negative short-term impact), but

at the end of December clear benefits were in evidence (greater diversity and less loss of income and jobs). In the end, the town appeared to be reinventing itself. The pastor of Edna, Rev. Andrew Schroer, concluded: "From my perspective, God provided. I truly believe that." I do not think God had anything to do with it; it had to do with the spirit of people rediscovering their identity and wanting to express it.

8   Goos, Manning, and Salomons, "Job polarization in Europe."

9   "Close to 60 Percent of Surveyed Tech Workers Are Burnt Out – Credit Karma Tops the List for Most Employees Suffering from Burnout," *Blind Blog – Workplace Insights*, 29 May 2018, https://www.teamblind.com/blog/index.php/2018/05/29/close-to-60-percent-of-surveyed-tech-workers-are-burnt-out-credit-karma-tops-the-list-for-most-employees-suffering-from-burnout/.

10 Blechter et al., "Correlates of Burnout," 529.

11 Ferris and West, "Economies of Scale."

12 Centers for Disease Control and Prevention, *The Relationship between Bullying and Suicide*.

13 The definition of a small country will always be somewhat arbitrary. It is a combination of the number of inhabitants and the surface area. A country with less than 20 million inhabitants is considered "small."

14 Gruebner et al., "Cities and Mental Health."

15 Sundquist and Sundquist, "Urbanisation and Incidence."

16 Abbott, "Stress and the City," 162. Urbanologists endeavour to take this into account when planning cities. Tokyo, for example, has tried to blend all layers of society in a neighbourhood. Mixing different amenities in a neighbourhood can also help. Finally, the car is a potential source of stress in cities, and insights into this are beginning to change.

17 Vries et al., "Natural Environments."

18 Randolph, "Children in the Compact City."

19 Evans, Lercher, and Kofler, "Crowding and Children's Mental Health."

20 Recsei, "Pipe Dreams," 68; Recsei, "Health, Happiness, and Density."

21 Jowell, Zhou, and Barry, "The Impact of Megacities on Health," e176–e178.

22 Andrade et al., "Mental Disorders in Megacities," 1.

23 Recsei, "Health, Happiness, and Density"; Lederbogen et al., "City Living"; Andrade et al., "Mental Disorders in Megacities," 1.

24 Recsei, "Health, Happiness, and Density."

25 Rosling, Rosling, and Rönnlund, *Factfulness*.

26 Some scientists consider that the YouTube version narrated by George Monbiot (*How Wolves Change Rivers*) about the transformation of

Yellowstone is not scientific. Yellowstone researchers, however, do not doubt the impact of wolves; only its further application is open to debate.

27   Twenty-five years after returning to Yellowstone, wolves have helped stabilize the ecosystem (nationalgeographic.com).

Chapter Six

1   "GDP Per Capita Growth (Annual %)," data for all countries and economies, 1961–2021, World Bank, https://data.worldbank.org/indicator/NY.GDP.PCAP.KD.ZG.

2   *White elephants* is a name for useless infrastructure works, for investments that have no economic use or whose maintenance cannot be borne. They are expensive investments compared to the potential economic return.

3   In bias to winners, performance is influenced by the winners, the best companies. The bad ones fall out of the index and are replaced by those that perform better. As a result, an index is mainly a composition of a small group of top companies and is not always a good indicator for all companies in an economy.

4   McCloskey notes that inequality has only increased in the United Kingdom, the United States, and Canada. Piketty claims that capitalism always makes the rich richer and the poor poorer. This is not true, however; it does not happen in all places, in all time periods after 1800. So Piketty is generalizing something that is impossible based on the facts he discovered. He also primarily examines physical capital, whereas today it is primarily about human capital. McCloskey notes that tremendous progress provided everyone with a far richer quality of life. Equality in rights and social dignity are major achievements that Piketty fails to mention. By pointing to excesses such as super-yachts or gold rings, Piketty blinds his readers and makes them fail to see the great social and economic achievements, thus running the risk of renouncing those achievements. Piketty's argument applies more to the United States than to Europe. Remove the rise of gigantism – and especially the tech giants – from the statistics, and things look altogether different. For a more complete overview of Piketty's errors, see McCloskey, "Measured, Unmeasured, Mismeasured, and Unjustified Pessimism," 73–115.

5   Gordon, "The Rise and Fall of American Growth."

6   Andrews, Criscuolo, and Gal, *The Best versus the Rest.*

7   Zuckoff, *Ponzi's Scheme*.
8   The difference between a pyramid scheme and a Ponzi scheme is subtle. In a pyramid scheme the investors themselves must attract new investors and motivate them to take their place; in a Ponzi scheme those managing the scheme assume that task.
9   Of course, this is meant ironically. The Nobel Prize in Economics was first awarded in 1969; Charles Ponzi died in 1949.

Chapter Seven

1   Recent studies and articles have cast considerable doubt on hospitals becoming cheaper as a result of economies of scale. The economic benefits are therefore not so obvious. Abelson, "When Hospitals Merge to Save Money."
2   Taleb, *Antifragile*.
3   This situation is magnified by big data. A lesson from Cathy O'Neil's book *Weapons of Math Destruction* is that centrally managed systems are using more "standardised rules." Such standardized rules are now being automated. Individuals are compared to what is right for the "average person." But something that is average for a group does not say much about an individual. With big data, this seems even more of an objective process because it is "maths and data." But inequalities and excesses become even more institutionalized, and it becomes more and more difficult to challenge them because "the system is right." The central system becomes a non-transparent, automated, impersonal process.
4   Kuhn and Morlino, "Decentralisation in Times of Crisis."
5   Greer et al., "Centralisation and Decentralisation in a Crisis."
6   Adolph Wagner (1835–1917) was a German economist.
7   Nassim Nicholas Taleb (@nntaleb), Tweet, 20 June 2016, 9:34 a.m., https://twitter.com/nntaleb/status/741262215949471749.
8   Soros is said to have gained USD 1 billion from the devaluation of the British pound.
9   Keegan, Marsh, and Roberts, "Six Days in September."
10 Since the great recession of 2008, the growth of world trade has slowed. Brexit and Trump, but also left-wing politicians in the United States and Europe, oppose globalization, which until 2008 had been rolled out without many impediments.
11 Weiner, *The Geography of Genius*.
12 Khanna, *Connectography*.

13 As already mentioned, megacities are not happy places. However, cities
    are not necessarily bad for human health; badly organized cities with
    too many excesses and too dense a population are.
14 Kohr, "Disunion Now," 94–8.
15 Taleb, *Antifragile*.

Chapter Eight

1   During the *ancien régime* a guild was an interest organization of
    people with the same profession. In some parts of the Netherlands,
    people used the term *crafts*. The guilds and trades existed from the
    Middle Ages until the end of the eighteenth century.
2   Political interest, more commonly known as rent-seeking, is an
    attempt to gain personal advantage through politics, or specifically
    lobbying, to the detriment of society.
3   The Paris Agreement, an international treaty on climate change, was
    adopted by 196 parties at COP 21 in Paris on 12 December 2015 and
    entered into force on 4 November 2016. "The Paris Agreement," United
    Nations Climate Change, accessed 13 January 2023, https://unfccc.int/
    process-and-meetings/the-paris-agreement/the-paris-agreement.
4   Anne Gallagher, "3 Reasons All Countries Should Embrace the
    Global Compact for Migration," World Economic Forum, 22 August
    2018, https://www.weforum.org/agenda/2018/08/3-reasons-all-
    countries-should-embrace-the-global-compact-for-migration/. Rik
    Van Cauwelaert wrote in *De Tijd* on 17 November 2018: "This puts
    the pact in line with the plea made years ago at the World Economic
    Forum in Davos to ease international migration. Some left-wing
    groups and parties even suspect that international business is using the
    global migration pact as a vehicle for the supply of (cheap) labour."
5   Prices are shown as of 2011. In 2014 all tariffs had already risen by
    20 per cent. So in 2019 the prices were probably at least a third higher.
6   Sorkin, "A Hefty Price for Entry to Davos."

Conclusions

1   Smith, *Theory of Moral Sentiments*.
2   Smith, *An Inquiry into the Nature*, 19.
3   Acemoglu and Robinson, *Why Nations Fail*, 529.

BIBLIOGRAPHY

Abbott, A. "Stress and the City: Urban Decay." *Nature News* 490 (7419): 162.

Abelson, Reed. "When Hospitals Merge to Save Money, Patients Often Pay More." *New York Times*, 14 November 2018. https://www.nytimes.com/2018/11/14/health/hospital-mergers- health-care-spending.html.

Acemoglu, D. *The Crisis of 2008: Structural Lessons for and from Economics.* MIT, 2009.

Acemoglu, Daron, and James A. Robinson. *Why Nations Fail: The Origins of Power, Prosperity and Poverty.* New York: Crown, 2012.

Affeldt, Pauline, and Kesler Reinhold. "Competitors' Reactions to Big Tech Acquisitions: Evidence from Mobile Apps." DIW Berlin Discussion Paper No. 1987. https://ssrn.com/abstract=3998875 or http://dx.doi.org/10.2139/ssrn.3998875.

Akcigit, Ufuk, and Sina T Ates. "What Happened to U.S. Business Dynamism?" National Bureau of Economic Research Working Paper Series No. 25756. http://www.nber.org/papers/w25756 or doi: 10.3386/w25756.

Andrade, L.H., Y.-P. Wang, S. Andreoni, C.M. Silveira, C. Alexandrino-Silva, E.R. Siu, et al. "Mental Disorders in Megacities: Findings from the São Paulomegacity Mental Health Survey, Brazil." *PLOS ONE* 7, no. 2. https://doi.org/10.1371/journal.pone.0031879.

Andrews, D., C. Criscuolo, and P.N. Gal, P. N. *The Best versus the Rest: The Global Productivity SlowDown, Divergence across Firms and the Role of Public Policy.* Paris: OECD Publishing, 2016.

Angotti, T., B. Paul, T. Gray, and D. Williams. *Wal-mart's Economic Footprint: A Literature Review Prepared by Hunter College Center for Community Planning & Development and New York City Public Advocate Bill de Blasio.* New York: Center for Community Planning and Development, Hunter College, 2010.

Arora, Ashish, Wesley M. Cohen, Honggi Lee, and Divya Sebastian. "Invention Value, Inventive Capability and the Large Firm Advantage." National Bureau of Economic Research Working Paper Series 30354, 2022. http://www.nber.org/papers/w30354 or doi: 10.3386/w30354.

Astebro, Thomas, Serguey Braguinsky, and Yuheng Ding. 2020. "Declining Business Dynamism among Our Best Opportunities: The Role of the Burden of Knowledge." National Bureau of Economic Research Working Paper Series 27787. http://www.nber.org/papers/w27787 or doi: 10.3386/w27787.

Autor, D., D. Dorn, L.F. Katz, C. Patterson, and J. Van Reenen, J. "The Fall of the Labor Share and the Rise of Superstar Firms." National Bureau of Economic Research Working Paper Series w23396. http://www.nber.org/papers/w23396.

Bajgar, Matej, Chiara Criscuolo, and Jonathan Timmis. "Intangibles and Industry Concentration: Supersize Me." OECD Science, Technology and Industry Working Papers 2021/12. Paris: OECD Publishing, 2021. https://doi.org/10.1787/ce813aa5-en.

Bernanke, B. *Essays on the Great Depression*. Princeton University Press, 2000.

Blechter, B., N. Jiang, C. Cleland, C. Berry, O. Ogedegbe, and D. Shelley. (2018). "Correlates of Burnout in Small Independent Primary Care Practices in an Urban Setting." *Journal of the American Board of Family Medicine* 31, no. 4: 529–36. https://doi.org/10.3122/jabfm.2018.04.170360.

Bordo, M.D., and L. Jonung. "The Future of EMU: What Does the History of Monetary Unions Tell Us?" National Bureau of Economic Research Working Paper w7365. http://www.nber.org/papers/w7365.

Borio, C. "A Blind Spot in Today's Macroeconomics?" Speech presented at BIS-IMF-OECD Joint Conference on Weak Productivity: The Role of Financial Factors and Policies, Paris, 10 January 2018.

– "Towards a Financial Stability-Oriented Monetary Policy Framework." Presentation at the conference held to mark the 200th anniversary of the Oesterreichische Nationalbank, 13–14 September 2016.

Borio, C.E., E. Kharroubi, C. Upper, and F. Zampolli. "Labour Reallocation and Productivity Dynamics: Financial Causes, Real Consequences." BIS Working Paper 534, 2016.

Bouman, Mathijs. "De wal keert het schip: Onze wereldeconomie loopt vast in gigantisme." *Het Financieele Dagblad*, 2021. https://fd.nl/opinie/1378437/de-wal-keert-het-schip-onze-wereldeconomie-loopt-vast-in-gigantisme-tzc1caFQlyyY.

Brynjolfsson, E., and A. McAfee. *Race against the Machine: How the Digital Revolution Is Accelerating Innovation, Driving Productivity, and*

Irreversibly Transforming Employment and the Economy. Lexington, MA: Digital Frontier Press, 2012.

Buyst, E., M. Goos, and A. Salomons. "Job Polarization: An Historical Perspective." *Oxford Review of Economic Policy* 34, no. 3: 461–74.

Cardiff-Hicks, B., F. Lafontaine, and K. Shaw. "Do Large Modern Retailers Pay Premium Wages?" *Industrial and Labor Relations Review* 68, no. 3: 633–65.

Cavalleri, Maria Chiara, Alice Eliet, Peter McAdam, Filippos Petroulakis, Ana Soares, and Isabel Vansteenkiste. "Concentration, Market Power and Dynamism in the Euro Area." ECB Working Paper 2019/2253. https://ssrn.com/abstract=3957695.

Cecchetti, S.G., and E. Kharroubi. "Reassessing the Impact of Finance on Growth." BIS Working Paper 381, 2012.

– "Why Does Financial Sector Growth Crowd Out Real Economic Growth?" CEPR Discussion Paper 490.

Centers for Disease Control and Prevention. *The Relationship between Bullying and Suicide: What We Know and What It Means for Schools.* Chamblee, GA: Centers for Disease Control and Prevention, National Center for Injury Prevention and Control, Division of Violence Prevention, 2014. https://www.cdc.gov/violenceprevention/pdf/yv/bullying-suicide-translation-final-a.pdf.

Coase, R.H. "The Problem of Social Cost." *Journal of Law & Economics* 3 (1960): 1–44. http://www.jstor.org/stable/724810.

Columbia Magazine. "What Do Retail Workers Want? Just a Little Respect." Winter 2018–19. https://magazine.columbia.edu/article/what-do-retail-workers-want-just-little-respect.

Corkery, Michael. "The Town That Lost Its Walmart." *New York Times*, 24 December 2019. https://www.nytimes.com/2019/12/24/business/walmart-edna-texas.html.

Courtemanche, C., and A. Carden. "Supersizing Supercenters? The Impact of Walmart Supercenters on Body Mass Index and Obesity." *Journal of Urban Economics* 69, no. 2: 165–81.

Cunningham, C., F. Ederer, and S. Ma. "Killer Acquisitions" *Journal of Political Economy* 129, no. 3: 649–702. https://doi.org/10.1086/712506.

Darmouni, Olivier, and Lira Mota. "The Savings of Corporate Giants." CEPR Discussion Paper DP17192. https://ssrn.com/abstract=4121367.

Diez, F.J., D. Leigh, and S. Tambunlertchai. "Global Market Power and Its Macroeconomic Implications." IMF Working Paper 18137, 15 June 2018. https://www.imf.org/en/Publications/WP/Issues/2018/06/15/Global-Market-Power-and-its-Macroeconomic-Implications-45975.

Döttling, R., G.G. Gallardo, and T. Philippon. "Is There an Investment Gap in Advanced Economies? If So, Why." Mimeo, 2017.

Draghi, M. "The Interaction between Monetary Policy and Financial
    Stability in the Euro Area." Speech at the First Conference on
    Financial Stability organized by the Banco de España and Centro de
    Estudios Monetarios y Financieros, Madrid, 24 May 2017.
Drehmann, M., C.E. Borio, and K. Tsatsaronis, K. "Characterising the
    Financial Cycle: Don't Lose Sight of the Medium Term." BIS Working
    Paper 380.
The Economist. "Dynamism Has Declined across Western Economies."
    15 November 2018. https://www.economist.com/special-report/2018/
    11/15/dynamism-has-declined-across-western-economies.
Evans, G.W., P. Lercher, and W.W. Kofler. "Crowding and Children's Mental
    Health: The Role of House Type." Journal of Environmental Psychology 22,
    no. 3: 221–31.
Ferris, J.S., and E.G. West. "Economies of Scale, School Violence and the
    Optimal Size of Schools." Applied Economics 36, no. 15: 1677–84. https://
    doi.org/10.1080/0003684042000266856.
Foster, Lucia S., John C. Haltiwanger, and Cody Tuttle. "Rising Markups or
    Changing Technology?" National Bureau of Economic Research Working
    Paper Series 30491. http://www.nber.org/papers/w30491 or doi: 10.3386/
    w30491.
Furman, J., and P. Orszag. "A Firm-Level Perspective on the Role of Rents in
    the Rise in Inequality." Presentation at "A Just Society" Centennial Event
    in Honor of Joseph Stiglitz, Columbia University, New York, 2015.
Giancotti, M., A. Guglielmo, and M. Mauro. "Efficiency and Optimal
    Size of Hospitals: Results of a Systematic Search." PLOS ONE 12, no. 3:
    e0174533. doi: 10.1371/journal.pone.0174533. PMID: 28355255; PMCID:
    PMC5371367.
Global Cities Institute. Socioeconomic Pathways and Regional Distribution of
    the World's 101 Largest Cities. Global Cities Institute, 2014.
Goos, M., A. Manning, and A. Salomons. "Job Polarization in Europe."
    American Economic Review 99, no. 2: 58–63.
Gordon, R.J. "The Rise and Fall of American Growth." In The Rise and Fall
    of American Growth: The U.S. Standard of Living since the Civil War.
    Princeton University Press, 2016.
Greer, Scott L., Michelle Falkenbach, Holly Jarman, Olga Löblová, Sarah
    Rozenblum, Noah Williams, and Matthias Wismar. "Centralisation and
    Decentralisation in a Crisis: How Credit and Blame Shape Governance."
    Eurohealth 27, no. 1: 36–40.
Griffin, Paul. The Carbon Majors Database: CDP Carbon Majors Report
    2017. CDP. https://cdn.cdp.net/cdp-production/cms/reports/

documents/000/002/327/original/Carbon-Majors-Report-2017. pdf?1501833772.

Gruebner, O., M.A. Rapp, M. Adli, U. Kluge, S. Galea, and A. Heinz. "Cities and Mental Health." *Deutsches Arzteblatt International* 114, no. 8 (2017): 121–7. doi: 10.3238/arztebl.2017.0121.

Grullon, G., Y. Larkin, and R. Michaely. "Are U.S. Industries Becoming More Concentrated?" *Review of Finance* 23, no. 4 (2019): 697–743. https://doi.org/10.1093/rof/rfz007.

Gutiérrez, Germán, and Thomas Philippon. "How EU Markets Became More Competitive Than US Markets: A Study of Institutional Drift." NBER Working Paper 24700.

Heede, R. "Tracing Anthropogenic Carbon Dioxide and Methane Emissions to Fossil Fuel and Cement Producers, 1854–2010." *Climatic Change* 122 (2014): 229–41. https://doi.org/10.1007/s10584-013-0986-y. https://link.springer.com/article/10.1007/s10584-013-0986-y?wptouch_preview_theme=enabled.

Illich, Ivan. *Deschooling Society*. New York: Harper & Row, 1971.

Jia, P. "What Happens When Wal-Mart Comes to Town: An Empirical Analysis of the Discount Retailing Industry." *Econometrica* 76, no. 6: 1263–316.

Johansson, Å., Ø.B. Skeie, S. Sorbe, and C. Menon. "Tax Planning by Multinational Firms." OECD Working Paper 1355. https://www.oecd.org/eco/Tax-planning-by-multinational-firmsfirm- level-evidence-from-a-cross-country-database. pdf.

Jowell, A., B. Zhou, and M. Barry. "The Impact of Megacities on Health: Preparing for a Resilient Future." *Lancet Planetary Health* 1, no. 5: PE176–E178.

Keegan, W., D. Marsh, and R. Roberts. *Six Days in September: Black Wednesday, Brexit and the Making of Europe*. OMFIF Press, 2017.

Kelton, Stephanie. *The Deficit Myth: Modern Monetary Theory and the Birth of the People's Economy*. Public Affairs, 2020.

– "How We Think about the Deficit." *New York Times*, 5 October 2017. www.nytimes.com/2017/10/05/opinion/deficit-tax-cuts-trump.html.

Khanna, P. *Connectography: Mapping the Future of Global Civilization*. Random House, 2016.

Kohr, Leopold. *The Breakdown of Nations*. London: Routledge & Paul, 1957.

– "Disunion Now: A Plea for a Society Based Upon Small Autonomous Units (1941)." *Telos*, 91 (1992): 94–8.

Koller, Tim, McKinsey & Company Inc., Marc Goedhart, and David Wessles. *Valuation: Measuring and Managing the Value of Companies*. Wiley, 2015.

Kroen, Thomas, Ernest Liu, Atif R. Mian, and Amir Sufi. "Falling Rates and Rising Superstars." National Bureau of Economic Research Working Paper Series 29368. http://www.nber.org/papers/w29368. doi:10.3386/w29368.

Krugman, Paul (2019) "What's Wrong with Functional Finance? (Wonkish): The Doctrine behind MMT Was Smart But Not Completely Right." *New York Times*, 12 February 2019. https://www.nytimes.com/2019/02/12/opinion/whats-wrong-with-functional-finance-wonkish.html.

Kuhn, Katharina, and Irene Morlino. "Decentralisation in Times of Crisis: Asset or Liability? The Case of Germany and Italy during Covid-19." *Swiss Political Science Review*, 8 October 2021. https://doi.org/10.1111/spsr.12482.

Kwon, Spencer, Yueran Ma, and Kaspar Zimmermann. "100 Years of Rising Corporate Concentration." SAFE Working Paper 359. https://ssrn.com/abstract=3936799. http://dx.doi.org/10.2139/ssrn.3936799.

Lederbogen, F., P. Kirsch, L. Haddad, F. Streit, H. Tost, P. Schuch, et al. "City Living and Urban Upbringing Affect Neural Social Stress Processing in Humans." *Nature* 474, no. 7352: 498–501.

Leonhardt, David. "The Charts That Show How Big Business Is Winning." *New York Times*, 17 June 2018. https://www.nytimes.com/2018/06/17/opinion/big-business-mergers.html.

Levinson, M. *The Box: How the Shipping Container Made the World Smaller and the World Economy Bigger*. Princeton University Press, 2006.

Lewis, A., and D. McKone. "So Many M&A Deals Fail Because Companies Overlook This Simple Strategy." *Harvard Business Review*, 20 May 2016, 1–5.

Loecker, Jan de, Jan Eeckhout, and Gabriel Unger. "The Rise of Market Power and the Macroeconomic Implications." *Quarterly Journal of Economics* 135, no. 2: 561–644. https://doi.org/10.1093/qje/qjz041.

Loecker, Jan de, Tim Obermeier, and John Van Reenen. "Firms and Inequality." *IFS Deaton Review of Inequalities*, 3 March 2022. https://ifs.org.uk/inequality/firms-and-inequality.

Manyika, James, Michael Birshan, Sven Smit, Jonathan Woetzel, Kevin Russell, and Lindsay Purcell. "A New Look at How Corporations Impact the Economy and Households." McKinsey & Company Discussion Paper, 31 May 2021.

Mazzucato, Mariana. *Mission Economy: A Moonshot Guide to Changing Capitalism*. Allen Lane, 2001.

– "Stop Whining About Big Government." *New York Times*, 15 March 2021.

McCloskey, D.N. *Bourgeois Dignity: Why Economics Can't Explain the Modern World*. Chicago: University of Chicago Press, 2016.

– *Bourgeois Equality: How Ideas, Not Capital or Institutions, Enriched the World.* Chicago: University of Chicago Press, 2016.
– *The Bourgeois Virtues: Ethics for an Age of Commerce.* Chicago: University of Chicago Press, 2006.
– "Measured, Unmeasured, Mismeasured, and Unjustified Pessimism: A Review Essay of Thomas Piketty's Capital in the Twenty-First Century." *Erasmus Journal for Philosophy and Economics* 7, no. 2: 73–115.
Medina, Alejandra, Adriana de la Cruz, and Yun Tang. "Corporate Ownership and Concentration." OECD Corporate Governance Working Paper 27. Paris: OECD Publishing, 2022. https://doi.org/10.1787/bc3adca3-en.
Miles, L., A. Borchert, and A.E. Ramanathan. "Why Some Merging Companies Become Synergy Overachievers." Bain & Company, 13 August 2014. https://www.bain.com/insights/why-some-merging-companies-become-synergy-overachievers.
Nguyen, H., and B.H. Kleiner. "The Effective Management of Mergers." *Leadership and Organizational Development Journal* 24, no. 8: 447–54.
OECD (Organisation for Economic Co-operation and Development). "Declining Business Dynamism: Cross-Country Evidence, Possible Drivers and the Role of Policy." Directorate for Science, Technology and Innovation Policy Note. Paris: OECD, Paris, 2021. www.oecd.org/sti/ind/declining-business-dynamism.pdf.
O'Neil, Cathy. *Weapons of Math Destruction: How Big Data Increases Inequality and Threatens Democracy.* Crown, 2017.
Phelps, E.S. "Corporatism and Keynes: His Philosophy of Growth." In *Revisiting Keynes: Economic Possibilities for Our Grandchildren*, ed. Lorenzo Pecchi and Gustavo Piga, 94–104. MIT Press, 2008. doi:10.7551/mitpress/9780262162494.003.0006.
Piketty, T. *Capital in the Twenty-First Century.* Cambridge, MA: Harvard University Press, 2014.
Randolph, B. "Children in the Compact City: Fairfield as a Suburban Case Study." Paper Commissioned by the Australian Research Alliance for Children and Youth. University of New South Wales, October 2006.
Raworth, K. *Doughnut Economics: Seven Ways to Think like a 21st-Century Economist.* Vermont: Chelsea Green Publishing, 2017.
Recsei, T. "Health, Happiness, and Density." NewGeography.com, 19 September 2013. http://www.newgeography.com/content/003945-health-happiness-and-density.
– "Pipe Dreams: The Shortcomings of Ideologically Based Planning." *People and Place* 13, no. 2: 68–81.

Ritholtz, Barry. "Apple Becomes the Largest Company Ever." Ritholtz.com,
     21 August 2012. https://ritholtz.com/2012/08/apple-becomes-the-
     largest-company-ever/.
Rosling, H., O. Rosling, and A.R. Rönnlund. *Factfulness: Ten Reasons We're
     Wrong about the World – And Why Things Are Better Than You Think.*
     St Martin's Press, 2018.
Salinas, Sara. "Amazon Raises Minimum Wage to $15 for All US Employees."
     CNBC, 2 October 2018. https://www.cnbc.com/ 2018/10/02/amazon-
     raises-minimumwage-to-15-for-all-us-employees.html.
Smith, A. *An Inquiry into the Nature and Causes of the Wealth of Nations.* 1776.
– *Theory of Moral Sentiments.* 1759.
Sorkin, Andrew Ross. "A Hefty Price for Entry to Davos." *New York Times,*
     24 January 2011. https://dealbook.nytimes.com/2011/01/24/a-hefty-
     price-for-entry-to-davos/.
Sundquist, K., G. Frank, and J. Sundquist. "Urbanisation and Incidence of
     Psychosis and Depression: Follow-Up Study of 4.4 Million Women and
     Men in Sweden." *British Journal of Psychiatry* 184, no. 4: 293–8.
Taleb, N.N. *Antifragile: Things That Gain from Disorder.* Random House, 2014.
– *The Black Swan: The Impact of the Highly Improbable.* New York: Random
     House, 2007.
Toplensky, Rochelle. "Multinationals Pay Lower Taxes than a Decade Ago."
     Financial Times, 11 March 2018. https://www.ft.com/content/2b356956-
     17fc-11e8-9376-4a6390addb44.
UEFA (Union of European Football Associations). *The European Club
     Footballing Landscape.* Ninth Club Licensing Benchmarking Report,
     Financial Year 2016. Union of European Football Associations, 2018.
Veugelers, Reinhilde. "Are European Firms Falling Behind in the Global
     Corporate Research Race?" *Policy Contribution,* no. 6 (April 2018).
     Bruegel. https://www.bruegel.org/sites/default/files/wp_attachments/
     PC-06_2018-110418.pdf.
Vries, S. de, R.A. Verheij, P.P. Groenewegen, and P. Spreeuwenberg. "Natural
     Environments – Healthy Environments? An Exploratory Analysis of
     the Relationship between Greenspace and Health." *Environment and
     Planning A* 35, no. 10: 1717–31.
Weiner, E. *The Geography of Genius: A Search for the World's Most Creative
     Places from Ancient Athens to Silicon Valley.* New York: Simon &
     Schuster, 2016.
Wolfe, S.E., and D.C. Pyrooz. "Rolling Back Prices and Raising Crime Rates?
     The Walmart Effect on Crime in the United States." *British Journal of
     Criminology* 54, no. 2: 199–221. https://doi.org/10.1093/bjc/azt071.

Wu, Tim. *The Curse of Bigness: Antitrust in the New Gilded Age*. Columbia
    Global Reports, 2018.
Yellowstone Science. "Celebrating 20 Years of Wolves." Yellowstone National
    Park, 13 July 2016. https://www.nps.gov/yell/learn/upload/yellowstone-
    science-24-1-wolves.pdf.
Zuckoff, Mitchell. *Ponzi's Scheme: The True Story of a Financial Legend*.
    New York: Random House, 2005.